Database Management and Control

Database Management and Control

Kenmore S. Braithwaite, Ph.D.
AKI Group, Inc.

Intertext Publications
McGraw-Hill Book Company

New York St. Louis San Francisco Auckland Bogotá
Hamburg London Madrid Mexico Milan Montreal
New Delhi Panama Paris São Paolo
Singapore Sydney Tokyo Toronto

Library of Congress Catalog Card Number 89-85733

10 9 8 7 6 5 4 3 2 1

ISBN 0-07-007253-1

Intertext Publications/Multiscience Press, Inc.
One Lincoln Plaza
New York, NY 10023

McGraw-Hill Book Company
1221 Avenue of the Americas
New York, NY 10020

Composed in Ventura Publisher by Context Publishing Services,
San Diego, CA

To Sheralyn, Eleanor, Glynne, Lambert, Don, Ron, Rickey, Nyan, Judaea, Janice, and Jonathan. All my nieces and nephews who have taken inspiration from my work.

Contents

Preface

The main objective of this book is to provide selected readings on some topics that are currently being highlighted in INFORMATION RESOURCE MANAGEMENT (IRM). This volume provides readers with information on traditional topics on data analysis; database design; database security, integrity, and privacy; and disaster recovery. In an attempt to make the volume a practical guide that can be used by database administrators, data administrators, and system designers, many approaches that can be readily implemented in the reader's database environment have been included.

As the title suggests, the volume provides information on some interrelated topics in IRM, but deals with them independently of each other. Thus, each chapter in the book is intended to stand alone, and any continuity between chapters is purely incidental. Therefore, the reader who is interested primarily in data analysis techniques would not have to read the chapter on database design in order to understand the issues of data analysis.

Chapter 1 introduces the concepts of data administration and database administration, showing that database administration is but a subset of data administration and that, although different, the two functions are used interchangeably by several researchers. Chapter 2 introduces various data analysis techniques and shows how these techniques are used in the development of database systems. Chapter 3 outlines a database design methodology that has been developed, tested, and implemented by a major public utility.

The chapters on database security, integrity, and privacy and protection mechanisms are a direct result of years of research and practical application in a large database environment.

Chapter 6 on management, planning, and control of the database environment is, again, a direct result of a strategic business systems plan conducted for a major insurance firm.

Chapters 7, 8, and 9 are results of case studies done in the various topics covered. The chapters on data dictionary concepts and design can be easily implemented in any database environment. Chapter 9 on business systems planning follows the outline of IBM on studies of this nature.

Chapter 10 discusses a method for developing a database architecture. This architecture is currently being used in an advanced office information systems environment. Chapter 11 introduces the CASE tool wave to the readers. This area of data processing is the fastest growing of any equivalent area.

Finally, the disaster recovery plan outlined in Chapter 12 is the result of a study on that subject for a large health maintenance organization. The chapter discusses an approach for developing an implementable disaster recovery plan in large organizations.

—Ken S. Brathwaite

Acknowledgments

I am grateful for the comments and suggestions I received from Vic Howard, Stanley Locbe, Francis Chin, and Joy Louise Weldon. The initial draft of this manuscript was ably typed by Jane Cuffy. Her efforts are appreciated.

— Ken S. Brathwaite

1

Concepts of Data Administration and Database Administration

This chapter introduces concepts that are pertinent to the proper understanding of the functions of data administration.

In the 1970s a certain degree of specialization in managing the data resource emerged from the data processing function. This specialization was referred to in two ways: data administration and database administration. Today, however, those names are used to describe two separate functions.

Data administration (DA) is the establishment and enforcement of policies and procedures for managing the company's data as a corporate resource. It involves the collection, storage, and dissemination of data as a globally administered and standardized resource.

Database administration (DBA) is a technical function which performs database design and development, provides education on database technology, provides support to users in operational data management-related activities, and may provide technical support for data administration.

Data administration and database administration are not the same, although several authors have used the terms interchangeably. This author prefers to define data administration as that function responsible for the total management of the enterprise's data resource. Thus, database administration is a subset of data administration.

1.1 Approach to Coverage of Topics

Although the emphasis of this book is on the functions and tasks conducted by the traditional data administration department of a typical organization, the DBA functions are highlighted in this chapter since that function is recognized as the older of the two.

The DA functions and activities will be listed here, but the reader should refer to Chapter 6 for more detailed coverage of data administration concepts.

1.2 Functions of Data Administration

Gillenson defines data administration (DA) as the custodianship, management, planning, and documentation of an enterprise's data. Minami indicates that the data administration function includes development and coordination of the policies, procedures, and plans for the capture, correction, storage, and use of data. It also serves to provide custody of the data and to coordinate data activities with systems developers and users.

The DA functions will include:

- Logical design of database system. This function produces a schema that shows which data fields should be grouped together to form records and files, and how they are related.
- Liaison to systems personnel during the application development process. The DA personnel will frequently communicate to systems personnel the changing requirements of the logical database design and those of the users.
- Training all relevant personnel in data administration concepts and techniques.
- Setting and monitoring standards for logical and physical database design, data dictionary development and content, and systems testing and acceptance.
- Design of documentation including data dictionaries.
- Promotion and allowing for interdepartmental data sharing.
- Resolution of data sharing conflicts.
- Setting up facilities to monitor data usage and obtaining authorization for usage.

1.3   Activities of Data Administration

The activities listed below are the various tasks that must be performed by DA in order to carry out the stated functions:

• Developing and enforcing policies governing data collection
• Developing tactical and strategic plans for data use
• Developing definitional requirements for data dictionary items
• Developing/enforcing naming conventions
• Controlling data integrity and security
• Identifying potential DB applications
• Planning the evolution of the enterprise database
• Identifying opportunities for data sharing
• Providing database education to the enterprise
• Providing primary input to the data dictionary
• Working with internal auditors in auditing the database
• Long-range planning for the enterprise's data resource
• Promoting security and privacy controls

1.4   Positioning of Data Administration Function

A considerable amount of research has been conducted to determine the effect of positioning of DA on its success and effectiveness. Some researchers have indicated that DA should be part of the traditional management information systems structures, whereas others are in favor of having DA placed outside the management information systems structure.

The author favors DA being placed outside the management information systems structure. DA is responsible for all of the corporation's data resource and planning for the effective management of that resource. This data resource should have the same status as finances, personnel, marketing, and production. Thus, for effective management and recognition of data as a resource, the DA function should be outside of management information systems and on par with the accounting, marketing, and production departments.

1.5   Reporting Level of Data Administration Function

Research has shown that the data administration manager reports to several levels of management in the organization. The smallest percentage of such managers report directly to the president or chief executive officer (CEO) of the organization. A larger percentage report to the officer one level below the president; e.g., a vice-president. The percentage of managers increased as the reporting level away from the president increased.

Kahn indicates that the form of the DA function was dependent on the reporting level of the chief information officer (CIO), to whom the DA reports, in respect to the president.

The author has determined that the success of the DA function depends upon the reporting level.

Gillenson has shown that one of the inhibitors to success of the DA function is that it is not high enough in the organization. Ideally, the DA function should report directly to the president, but never more than one level below.

1.6   Summary of Data Administration Function and Activities

Recent survey and research have shown that DA is involved in the following functions and activities:

- Logical database design (note that physical database design is done by DBA)
- Data security and privacy
- User relation and education
- Policy formulation
- Data dictionary design and maintenance
- Conflict resolution and data sharing disputes
- Promotion of auditing and monitoring of the database
- Total management of the database environment and data resource

1.7   Functions of Database Administration

Database administration is concerned with the technical aspects of managing the data resource rather than the administrative aspects. These technical aspects require expertise in a particular database management system (DBMS) and designing database logical and physical structures.

The DBA functions will include:

- Physical design of database systems
- Assisting in the negotiation for the acquisition of hardware and software to support the database management system (DBMS)

- Acting as a contact point for users experiencing problems with the DBMS and associated software
- Monitoring the performance of the DBMS and the individual transactions against the databases
- Assisting in the development of long-term plans to ensure that adequate hardware capacity and facilities are available to meet the requirements of new systems or expansions of existing systems
- Ensuring that physical database designs, and the manner in which relationships are chosen to be implemented and maintained, are such that the addition of new physical databases are readily achievable with minimum disruption to existing systems
- Ensuring the integrity of production data by seeing that controls are implemented to deny unauthorized access and that adequate validation procedures are included in all transactions
- Ensuring the security and privacy of data by seeing that controls are implemented to safeguard against threats to databases, libraries, and log tapes
- Providing test facilities in the form of DBMS hardware and software
- Researching new DBMS packages, procedures, standards, and other support facilities
- Developing documentation practices, procedures, and standards both for internal DBA use and for users who interface with DBA and the DBMS

1.8 Scope of DBA Functions

The following sections are intended to delineate the scope of DBA functions by identifying some of the main activities. These activities will include:

- Secure operation of DBMS
- Design of physical databases
- Identification and maintenance of physical database design and usage standards, guidelines, and policies
- Identification of hardware, software, and other facilities required to aid DBA in the performance of its duties
- Identification of education and training requirements for its staff
- Continual monitoring of its functions, objectives, responsibilities and authority, so that DBA can best serve the changing needs of the corporation and its various departments

1.9   Activities of Database Administration

The activities of DBA are grouped according to the major phases of system development, operation, and maintenance. These phases and activities are illustrated in Figure 1-1.

1.9.1   DBA Activities During Feasibility

Activities during this phase are concerned with planning for the new application and its development. The activities include:

- Facility capacity planning — For each new application a plan of additional hardware and software facilities must be developed. Also, the likely effect of the new application on the total DBMS performance must be estimated.
- Operations staff planning — Ensure that for all current and future systems the DBA function is adequately staffed.
- Development staff planning — DBA ensures that it has adequately trained staff to meet its short-term needs and to provide proper support to current and projected database system development.

1.9.2   DBA Activities During Definition

The activities during the definition phase are mainly centered on the development of data definitions and logical views. The DBA activities will be as follows:

- Familiarization — a process of familiarization with the contents of the detailed definitions, the application's logical views, and data dictionary.
- Review — DBA will, along with other teams, review the completed detailed definition documentation.

1.9.3   DBA Activities During Design

DBA activities during the design phase are concerned with the design of physical databases to meet the application requirements and the integration of common databases used by more than one system. The activities include:

Phases / Activities	Feasibility	Definition	Design	Implementation	Conversion	Operation	Maintenance	Performance reviews
	Facility Capacity Planning	Familiarization	Database Design	Performance Monitoring	Conversion Facility	Approval for System	Review of Database	Review Design Details
	Operations Staff Planning	Reviews	Simulation	Operation of DBMS Test Facility	Plan for Production System	Control of System	Changes to Environment	Review Program Logs
	Development Staff Planning		Access Guidelines			Monitoring	Changes due to Staff performance	Integrity Failure
			Review and Approval				Revision of Plans	Security and Audit Facilities
			Test Facility					Performance Data

Figure 1-1   Activities of DBA During Various Design Phases

- Database design — Develop a physical database design. DBA will consider several factors, such as performance requirements, data transaction volumes, integrity, security requirements, CPU and peripheral capacity, access methods, pointers, indexing and compression alternatives, and media storage.
- Simulation — Identification of the parameters that represent the characteristics of the new system and the parameters that represent the characteristics of the existing workload. The simulation should provide a measure of likely performance, a comparison of design alternatives, and a verification of capacity estimates.
- Access guidelines — Produce DBMS database access guidelines. The guidelines will define unit costs for access to each segment of the data base. Different costs are also defined for insert, delete, replace, and retrieve.
- Review and approval — Subject the physical database design and access guidelines to a formal review. The review should determine that the design reflects the requirements of the corporate view and any other relevant standards.
- Test facility — The provision of suitable test facilities for system development must be planned and implemented.
  These facilities include:

  — Data set space
  — Utility procedure
  — Special routines; e.g., randomizing and compression
  — Hardware and software resources
  — Staff resource

1.9.4 DBA Activities During Implementation

The main activities during the implementation phase are generation of the DBMS and monitoring the testing of the new system to identify weaknesses in the physical database design or failure to adhere to standards. These activities include:

- Monitoring the performance of programs during testing
  Factors examined will include:

  CPU usage
  I/O activity
  Storage size

Performance variations
Program conflicts for data

- Operation of DBMS test facility — involves the starting, monitoring of, restart and/or recovery when required, component backup, and submission and monitoring of batch jobs for the DBMS test system.

1.9.5   DBA Activities During Conversion

Activities during this phase are concerned with supporting the conversion process and preparation for operational running of the system. These activities include:

- Conversion facility — provide DBMS conversion facility; e.g., generate the DBMS system, allocate library and data set space, and documentation.
- Plan for production system — develop plan for final operation. These plans involve monitoring arrangements, staff training and education, backup and reorganization arrangements, and correction arrangements.

1.9.6   DBA Activities During Operation

The activities during operation will include:

- Approval for running the system
- Control of the system and all DBMS facilities
- Monitoring — continual monitoring of overall DBMS production systems performance and availability

1.9.7   DBA Activities During Maintenance

The activities during the maintenance phase will include:

- Review of database and program changes
- Changes to the environment due to general hardware and software changes, DBMS changes, and tuning the DBMS
- Changes due to the performance of the DBA staff, revision of internal plans, and standards

1.9.8   DBA Activities During Performance Reviews

The activities during this phase will consist primarily of providing required information for any performance review including

- Design details
- Problem logs
- Integrity and security failures
- Audit facilities
- Performance data

1.10   Summary

This chapter has served to introduce the basic concepts of data administration (DA) and database administration (DBA). The most important concept highlighted the functions and activities of both areas.

The DBA activities were classified into phases corresponding to the development life cycle of systems. Each activity of DA was listed although not classified as above.

Finally, the coverage of the positioning and reporting level of the data administration function reported the results of industry research in those areas.

2

Data Analysis Techniques

This chapter introduces techniques for conducting data analysis and utilizing these techniques in development of database systems.

Data analysis is defined as the determination of the fundamental data resources of an organization. It deals with the collection of the basic entities and the relationships between those entities.

The chapter begins with definitions for terms generally used in data analysis. Such terms as data, data item, entity, attribute, and relationship are defined. It establishes the premise that data is a resource in much the same way as employees, products, natural resources, and finances are. It continues by discussing components of data analysis and techniques for performing normalization of data.

2.1 Definitions and Terminologies

Data Item The smallest unit of named data. A data item is often referred to as a field or data element.

Data The values taken by various data items. For example, the value of the data element Customer Name is data.

Information Data that is processed, accessed, and assimilated or used in the decision-making process. It is the analysis and synthesis of data.

Entity (or Entity Class or Entity Type) A fundamental thing of interest to an organization. An entity may be a person, place, thing, concept, or event, real or abstract. It should have a unique identifier.

Attribute A descriptive value or property associated with an individual entity.

Relationship An association between two or more entities.

Entity Model (Snap shot) A diagrammatical representation of the relationships between the entity classes. The representation allows us to include only those entities that are required to solve the user's data processing problem. It depends on the relationships you are concerned with.

Logical Schema (External Structure/Schema) The mapping of the entity model into the constructs or constraints of the database management system (DBMS). In general, the logical schema indicates how the model will be stored and accessed.

Data Analysis The determination of the fundamental data resources of an organization. It deals with the collection of the basic entities and the relationships between those entities.

2.2 Data as a Resource

Data must be seen as a resource in much the same way as employees, products, natural resources, finances, and other material products or resources. Data as a resource must be recognized to have cost and value. In order to exploit the data resource, it must be understood, conserved, employed, and integrated. It is necessary to learn about its nature and characteristics, how it is used, what it is used for, where it resides, and where it comes from.

2.2.1 Information Resource Management

Information resource management (IRM) deals with planning for, allocating, maintaining and conserving, prudently exploiting, effectively employing, and integrating the data resource.

To manage data effectively as a resource, it is necessary to obtain as much information about the data as is possible. There must be stringent procedures for collecting, maintaining, and using the resource.

2.2.2   Management Control of the Data Resource

Management control of data includes the following:

* Common procedures for access control to the data
* Establishing lines of authority and responsibility for the data
* Common procedures for collecting, updating, and maintaining the data
* Common formats and procedures for data definition
* Identifying entities that are important to the enterprise
* Evaluating, mediating, and reconciling the conflicting needs and prerogatives of functional departments
* Ensuring the auditability of the data and all transactions against the data
* Controlling the data in order to measure and evaluate the corporation and predict its reaction to changes in its environment and in its own internal organization

2.2.3   Data Ownership Philosophies

The introduction of the database era meant a change not only in traditional data processing, but also in traditional definitions of "data ownership." In traditional data processing, total control over creation, maintenance, and processing of data meant "ownership" of that data. In a database environment, data sharing and data integration has lessened total control and now imply loss of "ownership." In data analysis, the establishing of data "owners" is important to:

* Control access to the data
* Allow data sharing
* Establish relationships and interfaces between entities
* Establish common definitions for data
* Resolve discrepancies and conflicts over standards and conventions

2.2.4   Different Views of Data

Data about an enterprise is not singularly determined. Different people perceive and describe an enterprise differently, and hence have different starting points concerning what is to be modeled.

It's not merely a matter of scope, of including more or less in the view. People looking at the same thing *see* it differently.

Examples of Different Views of Data

- The secretary of a department may be, in someone else's view, the secretary of the manager of the department.
- A manufacturing operation might be performed by a certain department, or we might view it as performed by a person assigned to that department.
- A social security number is generally considered to identify a person, but it really identifies an account that belongs to a person.

2.3   Data Analysis

The primary purpose of data analysis is to determine the fundamental nature of an organization's data resources, and to organize and document all relevant facts concerning this data.

Data analysis has been used to:

- Determine the fundamental data resources of an organization
- Provide a disciplined approach toward cataloging the existing data in terms of the entities and relationships it represents
- Provide an effective means of communicating with non-data processing users, as it deals only with things that the users are familiar with and not with such objects as files and records
- Analyze the inherent structure of that data independently from the details of the applications
- Form a basis for data control, security, and auditing systems
- Organize all relevant facts concerning the organization's data
- Produce a point of reference (the Entity Model) against which a logical database structure for each of the database management systems can be designed
- Provide a sound basis for database design

2.3.1 Components of Data Analysis

Data analysis is regarded as consisting of two dependent projects:

1. *Entity analysis*, which provides a means of understanding and documenting a complex environment in terms of its entities and their attributes and relationships.
2. *Functional analysis*, which is concerned with understanding and documenting the basic business activities of the organization (Figure 2-1).

2.4 Requirements Analysis

Requirements Analysis involves:

- Establishment of organizational objectives
- Derivation of specific database requirements from those objectives or directly from management personnel
- Documentation of those requirements in a form that is agreeable to management and database designers (Figure 2-2)

2.4.1 Techniques Used in Requirements Analysis

- Personal interviews with various levels of management and key employees involved in the processing of goods, services, and data in the organization
- Diagramming of the flow process with which each employee is involved
- Identify the data elements associated with that process and the interfaces between processes
- Verification that both interviewer and employee agree on the flow model

2.5 User View Modeling

User view modeling is defined as the modeling of the usage and information structure perspectives of the real world from the point of view of different users and/or applications.

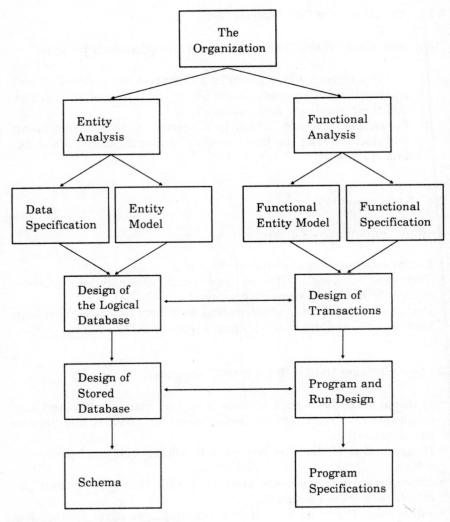

Figure 2-1   Analysis and Design

View modeling involves at least the following two components:

1. Extracting from the users or from persons in charge of application development the relevant parts of real-world information
2. Abstracting this information into a form which completely represents the user view so that it can be consequently used in database design

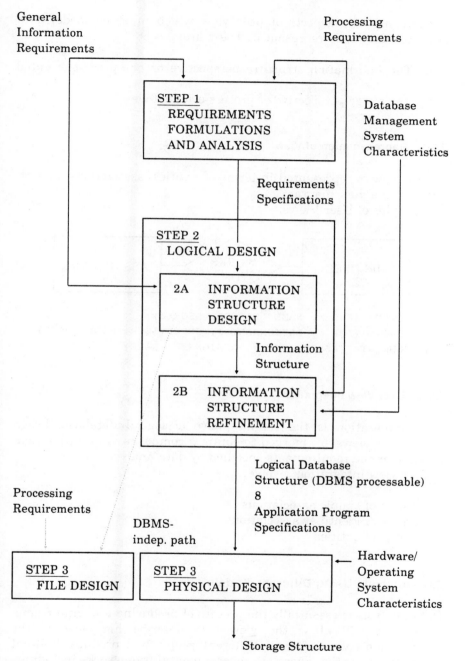

Figure 2-2   Basic Database Design Steps

There are two aspects of user view which must be modeled in order to adequately represent it. These are:

1. The information structure perspective or non-process-oriented view
2. The usage perspective or process-oriented view

2.5.1   Representation of View

A user view is represented in terms of entities, associations, and attributes in a view diagram.

Examples of User Views:

```
EMPLOYEE= {EMP #, NAME, SCHOOL, DEGREE}
WORKS-ON= {EMP #, ASSIGNMENT #, SUPERVISOR, START-DATE}
ASSIGNMENT= {ASSIGNMENT #, ASSIGNMENT-NAME}
```

2.5.2   User View Integration

View integration is the second phase of logical database design where user views are merged to obtain a composite view of the organization or the requirements specified by data analysis.

User view integration involves:

• Merging of simple associations
• Merging of identifier associations
• Merging of entities

2.6   Analysis Using Different Models

Data analysis is essentially the process of producing a mental framework that will allow the viewer to describe his view or the organization's view of data. Different people will produce different mental frameworks. There are several mental frameworks including:

• Data-structure diagrams
• Entity-relationship (E-R) model

2.6.1   Analysis Using Data-Structure Diagrams

Analysis using data-structure diagrams involves record types and data-structure sets, which are relationships between record types.

In Figure 2-3A, there are two types of conceptual records, COMPANY and PERSON, and a data-structure set representing the fact that each person is associated with exactly one company and that each company has a set of personnel.

Analysis may indicate that the personnel of the company were persons in their own right. This fact may be discovered at the merger of several companies that some of the personnel held two jobs and were personnel to two of the merged companies (Figure 2-3B). Basically, the old personnel type record has been split into two record types, PERSONNEL and PERSON.

Further analysis may indicate that the address of residence should not be in the person's record. This requires the creation of a PLACE conceptual record type and a new data-structure-set type (Figure 2-3C). It must be assumed that each person has a unique address.

It is now recognized that people move from place to place and that it is desirable to know current address as well as past addresses. Another reason may be that a person may have more than one address. In either case, a new conceptual record type ADDRESS is added to the structure (Figure 2-3D).

2.6.2   Analysis Using Entity-Relationship Diagrams

In the following, we shall use entity-relationship (E-R) diagrams to explain the above example in which data-structures were used.

The E-R diagram (Figure 2-4A) corresponds to the data-structure diagram in Figure 2-3A. There are two types of entities, PERSON and COMPANY, in the user view. The data-structure set is replaced by the relationship set WORKS FOR.

Analysis shows that a new entity PLACE should be introduced into the schema. Since many persons can have the same address, a new entity is introduced called ADDRESS. The final E-R diagram is detailed in Figure 2-4B.

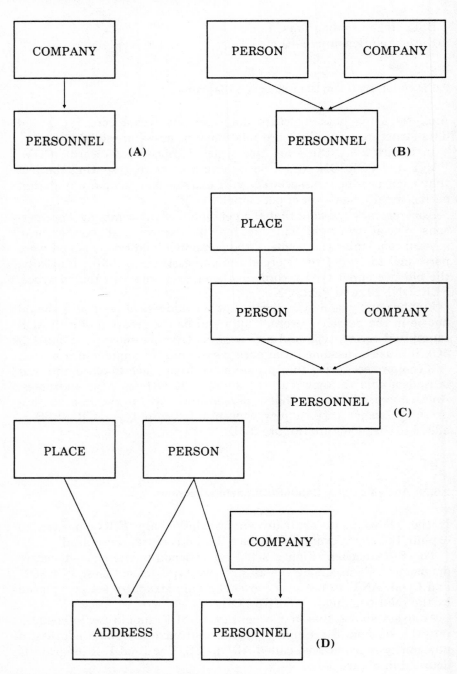

Figure 2-3   Analysis Using Data Structures

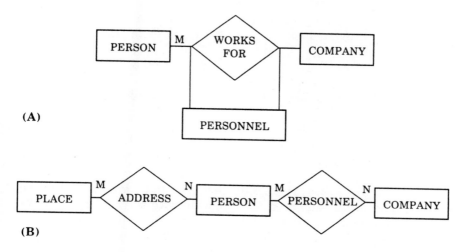

Figure 2-4

In general, the E-R diagram is easier to use to analyze the changes in the user view than data-structure diagrams.

It should be noted that the relationship WORKS FOR can be materialized into an entity called PERSONNEL. Similarly, the relationship LIVES AT can be materialized into an entity called ADDRESS.

2.7 Functional Analysis

Functional analysis is concerned with an understanding and documentation of the basic business activities with which the organization is concerned. Functional analysis has the following objectives:

- To determine how entities are used so as to increase understanding of the entity model
- To provide a firm basis for transaction design
- To gather estimates of data usage for database design

Functional analysis may reveal attribute types of entities not detected during entity analysis. Similarly, relationships between entities not previously considered meaningful may be found to be required by certain functions.

The basic functions identified in functional analysis would be expected to be translated into transaction types in the data processing system.

Estimates of data usage will provide a means for determining which access paths should be made most efficient.

Functional analysis can be divided into the following phases:

• Preliminary
• Develop a framework
• Access path analysis

In functional analysis the application area to be analyzed must be defined. The application area may coincide with the data area examined in data analysis, or it may cross several data areas. Here data area may be defined as the data utilized in areas determined by the organizational structure; e.g., accounting, personnel, manufacturing, marketing, and purchasing.

In the process of developing a framework, the analyst identifies the events and functions. Typically, there is a hierarchy of functions, but the basic activities at the foot of the hierarchy are initiated by events recurring in the organization.

An event may be defined as a stimulus to the organization, and functions may be defined as tasks that must be carried out as a direct result of the event.

For example, *an order is placed* is an event, whereas *record the order* or *produce the invoice* are functions.

2.7.1   Functional Analysis Example

One of the functions identified as being carried out in the order processing area is *order entry*. An order is received from a DELIVERY POINT. The depot that will make the delivery is selected depending on whether the goods are bulk or packaged. The order is recorded and related to the delivery point and the depot. The goods specified in each order line are validated and the stocks of the goods on hand are amended. Where stocks are insufficient to meet the quantities in one or more lines on the order, a backorder is created.

The order lines are recorded and linked to the goods and to the order, or backorder as appropriate.

The functional entity model resulting from the above description is shown in Figure 2-5.

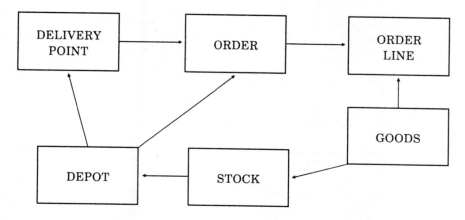

Figure 2-5   Functional Entity Model for Order Entry

2.8   Data Analysis Documentation

An essential outcome of data analysis is the documentation for entity types, relationship types, attribute types, functions, and events. *This documentation is in addition to the entity model and functional entity model.* Where the volumes and complexity are low, a clerical system has been found to be adequate, but in the longer term and in a dynamic environment, the use of a good data dictionary is advisable.

2.8.1   Data Analysis Documentation Examples

An example of a data dictionary that makes the distribution between the constructs of the entity model and those of the logical database and between the functions of the organization and the transactions which handle them will be discussed in another section.

Examples of the types of forms that could be employed for a clerical system of documentation for data analysis are shown below. The forms are used to document an entity, an attribute, and a relationship.

For functional analysis, the access path is documented. In addition, while no information concerning attributes is included in the functional entity model, the grouping of attributes as needed by different functions is normally shown in an attribute usage matrix, where for each entity the attributes are matched against the functions which retrieve, modify, store, or delete their values.

DATA ANALYSIS DOCUMENTATION ENTITY TYPE	ANALYST: K. Brathwaite
NAME: Order	DATE: 22.11.83 VERSION: 1 STATUS: Preliminary
SYNONYMS:	(Final)

DEFINITION: Request for delivery of a stated number of different goods

IDENTIFIERS: Order Number

OCCURRENCES:
MINIMUM   AVERAGE 240,000 per year   MAXIMUM

SPECIAL VARIATIONS: GROWTH: 10% per year

AUTHORIZED TO
CREATE: Order   DELETE: Order   COUNT: Marketing Processing   Processing   Research Department   Department

CONFIDENTIALITY: Types 3   SECURITY:

ENTITY SUBTYPES: Filled Order Back Order	IDENTIFIERS: F B

DEFAULT FOR ATTRIBUTE DETAILS: AVAILABILITY TIMELINESS STORAGE

Figure 2-6   Data Analysis Documentation—Entity Type

Similarly, the entity usage matrix summarizes overall functions the way a particular entity is accessed, whether by value of a particular attribute or by means of relationships. (See Figures 2-6, 2-7, 2-8.)

DATA ANALYSIS DOCUMENTATION ATTRIBUTE TYPE	ANALYST: K. Brathwaite
NAME: Credit Limit	DATE: 22.11.83
SYNONYMS:	VERSION: 1 STATUS: Preliminary
DEFINITION: If the customer's balance exceeds this value no further orders wil	
be accepted unless paid in advance.	
ENTITY DESCRIBED: Customer	
AUTHORIZED TO CREATE: Accounts Receivable MODIFY: Finance RETRIEVE: Salesman	
PERMITTED VALUES $10,000 to MEANING: FORMAT: 5 numeric digits RANGE: $25,000	
CONSISTENCY: Only for customers with over 3 AVAILABILITY: previous orders On-line	
STORAGE: TIMELINESS: Updated daily	

Figure 2-7   Data Analysis Documentation—Attribute Type

2.9   The Entity Model

The major output of the data analysis phase of database design is the entity model. The entity model is a diagrammatical representation of the relationships between the entities. The representation allows us to include only those entities that are required to solve the particular data processing problem.

The entity model is essentially a real-world view of the data in terms of entities, attributes, and relationships.

The model is used by the data analysis team to:

• Reduce redundancy in the relationships
• Determine which entities are significant to the model and the requirement of the problem

DATA ANALYSIS DOCUMENTATION RELATIONSHIP TYPE	ANALYST: K. Brathwaite
NAME: Places	DATE: 22.11.83
SYNONYMS:	VERSION: 1 STATUS: Preliminary

DEFINITION: The customer has indicated by phone or by mail that he wishes to buy a product

RELATED TO ENTITY: Order	ENTITY: Delivery Point

AUTHORIZED TO
CONNECT: Order Processing
              Department
	DISCONNECT: Order Processing
	                    Department

CONFIDENTIALITY: Type 3	

CONSISTENCY:	AVAILABILITY: On-line

REPRESENTATION:
    Contiguity in the customer file
	TIMELINESS:
	    Update daily

Figure 2-8(A)   Data Analysis Documentation—Relationship Type

Once the entity model is produced, the analysis team sets about the task of making revisions to the model.

This is done in order to:

• Produce the optimum model
• Normalize the entities
• Synthesize the relationships

2.10   Entity Model Production

The entity model can be produced using either a bottom-up or top-down approach. The bottom-up approach produces a composite or global view of the organization's data based on the integration of several user views of the immediate problems requirements and not

FUNCTIONAL ANALYSIS DOCUMENTATION							
ACCESS PATH							

FUNCTION NAME: Order Entry   REPONSE REQUIRED   5 sec 10 sec   Avg Max   ANALYST: KSB   DATE: 22.11.83

FREQUENCY ASSUMPTIONS: Per Day   Avg: 4000   Max: 6000   Growth: 10% per year

Entity (E) Relationship (R) Accessed	E/R	Selection Criteria	Action	Volume Avg	Max
Delivery Point	E	Delivery Point Name	R	1	1
Bulk/Package	R	Bulk/Packaged	R	1	1
Depot	E	Via Relationship	R	1	1
Order	E		S	1	1
Order/Delivery Point	R	Order No. Delivery Point Name	Con	1	1
Order/Depot	R	Order No. Depot Name	Con	1	1
Goods	E	Goods Code	R	10	30
Goods/Stock	R	Goods Code	R	10	30
Depot/Stock	R	Depot Name	R	10	30
Stock	E	Depot/Goods	M	9.5	28.5
Back Order	E	Back Order No.	S	0.5	1.5
Order/Delivery Point	R	Back Order No. Delivery Point Name	Con	0.5	1.5
Order/Depot	R	Back Order No. Depot Name	Con	0.5	1.5
Order Line	E	Order No. Goods Name	S	10	30

ACTION (ENTITY) RETRIEVE, MODIFY, STORE, DELETE ACTION (RELATIONSHIP), RETRIEVE, CREATE, CONNECT, DISCONNECT

Figure 2-8(B) Data Analysis Documentation—Relationship Type

on the inherent structure of the data. The resulting model is limited to the immediate problem and cannot reflect the entire business activities of the corporation.

The top-down approach produces a global, corporate, or organizational view of the data before the application views are identified. The entities and relationships of interest to the organization are

FUNCTIONAL ANALYSIS DOCUMENTATION				
SUMMARY OF ACCESS TO AN ENTITY TYPE				
ENTITY NAME: Goods TIME PERIOD: Per Day ANALYST: KSB DATE: 22.11.83				

DIRECT ACCESS		FREQUENCY OF ACCESS		
ATTRIBUTES	SELECTION CRITERIA	RETRIEVE AVG MAX	STORE AVG MAX	DELETE AVG MAX
DESCRIPTION	GOODS CODE	8×10^4 10^5	50 100	
UNIT OF ISSUE	GOODS CODE		10 15	
COST PRICE	GOODS CODE	260 300	50 80	
SALES PRICE	GOODS CODE	8×10^4 10^5	50 100	

VIA RELATIONSHIP		ACTION PERFORMED		
RELATIONSHIP	SELECTION CRITIERIA	RETRIEVE AVG MAX	TRANSFER AVG MAX	CONNECT AVG MAX
Stock/Goods	Goods delivered	4×10^4 5×10^4	20 30	
Order Line/Goods	Goods of amended			
Order Line/Goods	order		80 100	
	Goods of cancelled order			

Figure 2-8(C)   Data Analysis Documentation—Attribute Type

identified from the business activities of the total organization and independent of any particular application.

The bottom-up approach is the one most often used in data analysis. This approach produces a model with more clearly defined boundaries than the top-down approach. The processing requirements can be used by the data analysis team to precisely determine what entities are required and the composition of those entities. The clustering of attributes into their respective entities or the splitting of entities can be done with more precision. It is easier with this approach to determine whether an attribute is indeed an attribute of an existing entity or is itself an entity with relationships to other entities.

2.11 Translation of User View to Entity Model (MAPPING)

A significant difficulty in defining the relationships and representing them in the entity model is determining which relationships are directly significant and which are redundant. This can be done only with a detailed understanding of the environment, as there are no mathematical rules that can be applied but merely patterns in the entity model which prompt further investigation.

To determine the existence of relationships, the following procedure can be employed:

- Take each attribute type and determine which entity type it describes, whether it could describe any other entity type and if these entity types are related.
- Take each entity type and pair it with another and determine if a meaningful question can be asked.
- Determine if the relationship is relevant.

No less difficult is the decision concerning each element, as to whether it should be treated as an attribute type of an entity type or as a second entity type related to the first. As a guideline it has been found that an attribute of an entity-1 is best treated instead as entity-2 related to entity-1 if:

- The attribute itself is found to have further relevant attributes
- The resulting entity-2 is itself of significance to the organization
- The attribute in fact identifies entity-2
- Entity-2 could be related to several occurrences of entity-1
- Entity-2 is seen to be related to entity types other than entity-1

Thus in Figure 2-9, customer location is seen not to be an attribute of customer, as a customer may have several locations and as each location has its own attributes, such as postal code.

During the translation of the user view to the entity model, the most significant entity types and relationship types are defined. But inevitably a model will be extended or modified during the detailed data analysis phase as a result of reexamining the attributes.

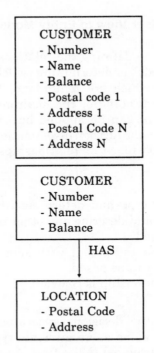

Figure 2-9   Replacing Attributes by Entities and Relationships

2.12   Selection and Identification of Entities

Data analysis permits the selection and identification of entities in the following three ways:

• By one or more attributes
• By the combination of a relationship with one or more attributes
• By two or more relationships

The simplest case of entity identification is where each occurrence of the attribute has a unique value which is used to identify the entity. Combinations of attributes may also be used, such as when employees are identified by their name, together with the date they joined the company.

The members of the relationship are often uniquely identified within that relationship by the values of the attribute type, but for uniqueness within the system the owner of the relationship needs also to be known. In effect, it is the relationship occurrence as identi-

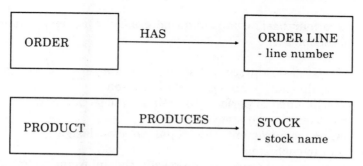

Figure 2-10   Entity Identification by Relationships

fied by its owner that contributes to the unique identification of its members. Entity identification by relationships and attributes is illustrated in Figure 2-10.

2.13   Entity Subtypes

A problem arises when different functions wish to use clearly identifiable subsets of the total population as attributes of an entity type. The question then arises as to whether the entity type, as defined, is taking too global a view and is better considered as being several entity types. In general it may be preferable to treat entities as being of different types if they have either:

- Significant differences in their attributes
- Different means of identification
- Participation in different types of relationships

2.14   Schema Development

The process of developing a database structure from user requirements is called database design. The database process consists of two phases:

- Design of a logical database structure (schema development) that is processable by the database management system (DBMS) and describes the user's view of the data
- Selection of a physical structure (physical database design) that is available within the DBMS

There are four basic components necessary to achieve a database design methodology:

• A structured design process that consists of a series of design steps where one alternative among many is chosen
• Design techniques to perform the required selection and evaluation of alternatives at each step
• Information requirements for input to the design process as a whole and to each step
• A descriptive mechanism to represent the information input and the results at each design step.

The result of the logical design step is a database definition or schema.

2.15   Formulating the DBMS — Specific Logical Database Schema

Using the entity-relationship diagrams developed during the user view modeling phase of database design, a processing matrix which links specific applications and entities identified in the processing requirements, and allowable DBMS characteristics, a logical database schema can be formulated.

In the simplest case, entities become record types and attributes become item types or entities become logical databases.

In the more complex cases, entities can split or merge to form record types. This step begins the phase where consideration of the DBMS-specific rules and constraints must be given.

2.16   Refining the Logical Database Schema for Processing Considerations

The logical database schema can now be revised on the basis of quantitative information and performance measures.

Processing volume is defined as the combination of two parameters:

• Processing frequency
• Data volume

Processing frequency is the frequency at which an individual application is required to be run.

Data volume is the number of occurrences of each record type currently stored or to be stored in the database.

Performance measures at the logical design step are limited to:

• Logical record access counts
• Total bytes transferred to satisfying an application
• Total bytes in the database

These measures attempt to predict physical database performance in terms of elapsed time and physical storage space as closely as possible.

2.17   Documenting the Database Design

Documentation is the recording of facts about objects or events of concern to facilitate communication and to provide a permanent record.

In a database environment, documentation is based on giving information about the database itself, its contents and its structure. The documentation focuses primarily on data-related components, such as:

• Data elements
• Data groups (records or segments)
• Data structures
• Databases

Database documentation covers several types of information and is intended to support the needs of several classes of users.

Seven types of documentation can be compiled for the database environment:

1. Name/Meaning — a unique identifier and descriptive information that conveys the full meaning of the component. The name is used for reference and retrieval purposes, while the description is valuable to managers and users
2. Physical description — the physical characteristics of the components, such as the size of a data element or the length of a data record
3. Edit/Authorization criteria — criteria to be used to test the validity of instances of the component, such as acceptable range

of values for data elements or passwords for update of a data base.

4. Usage — information on where and by whom or by what a component is used, such as the programs within a system that reference a given data element

5. Logical description — the characteristics and structure of each user view of the database, such as logical relationships among data records

6. Procedures — guidelines for human interaction with the database, such as backup, recovery, and system restart

7. Responsibility — a record of the individual or organizational unit responsible for the generation and maintenance of the database component

2.18   The Role of Data Dictionary/Directory Systems

Data dictionary directory (DD/D) systems are valuable tools for assisting generally in the collection and management of data about the database. This data about the database is called metadata.

The major objective of a DD/D system is to support the integration of metadata in much the same way that a DBMS supports the integration of an organization's data.

The benefits achieved are as follows:

• Minimum redundancy
• Consistency
• Standardization
• Data sharing
• Monitoring of database content
• Effectively enforcing security and integrity policies

2.19   Features and Functions of DD/D Systems

All data dictionary/directory systems provide the basic functions necessary to capture and maintain metadata and to generate reports from that store of metadata. Data capture implies the initial loading of the data dictionary with metadata of entry types. This capability may be provided through fixed — or free — format transactions in either batch or online mode. Very often, all or part of a data dictionary entry may be generated directly from source program data descriptions.

Reporting is a primary function of any DD/D system. Basically two types of reports are provided:

- List of dictionary entries, either alphabetically or by entry type
- A cross-reference report

In a cross-reference report entries in the dictionary are associated by the relationships in which they participate. Since these relationships are bidirectional, the cross-reference may be either top-down or bottom-up. For example, one may ask to see a top-down listing of entries associated with a particular application or might ask for a trace of all entries with which a particular element is associated, a bottom-up view.

Other DD/D system features may include:

- Selectivity — entries associated with a particular element
- Query languages — for users to formulate reports of their own choosing
- Program code generation
- Directory — indicating the physical location of data in the database
- Maintenance of archival definitions

2.20   The Normalization Process

During data analysis the relevant attributes are recorded and defined for each entity type. This may lead to identification of new entity types or to the subdivision of existing entities. It also enables the boundaries of the data area to be defined more precisely. Once the entity model is reasonably complete, explicit checks need to be made to detect redundant relationships. These checks may include the process called normalization.

2.20.1   Normalization

Normalization requires three actions to be performed on the attributes of an entity. These are as follows:

- First normal form — repeating groups are removed
- Second normal form — attributes are removed which are dependent on only some of the identifying attributes

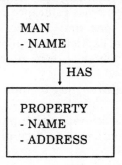

REMOVAL OF REPEATING GROUPS

Figure 2-11   First Normal Form

• Third normal form — any attributes are removed which are not directly dependent upon the identifying attributes

2.20.2   First Normal Form

During data analysis *man* was identified as one of the entity types of interest to the organization, and *address* was identified as one of the attributes of *man*. During the first normalization process it will be shown that there are hidden relationships inside the entity type since several men may reside at the same address or a man may have several addresses.

First Normal Form normalization would produce a new entity type *property* (say). (See Figure 2-11.)

2.20.3   Second Normal Form

A normalized relation (entity) is said to be in second normal form if all its nonprime attributes (attributes that do not serve to identify

the relation) are fully functionally dependent on each candidate key (attributes that uniquely identify the relation).
Example:

CUSTOMER	(ORDER #	CUSTOMER #	CUSTOMER NAME)
	1	241	H. Pratt
	2	250	M. Hall
	3	241	H. Pratt

In the above example, the nonprime attribute CUSTOMER NAME is fully dependent on the candidate key, ORDER #. That is, for each value of ORDER #, there is one and only one value of CUSTOMER NAME.
Unnormalized Relation:

CUSTOMER	(ORDER #	ITEM CODE	UNIT PRICE	QUANTITY)
	1	A10	5	10
	1	C13	3	20
	2	A10	5	15
	2	B16	12	2
	3	B16	12	11

In the above unnormalized relation, the attribute UNIT PRICE is not fully dependent on the candidate key ORDER #/ITEM CODE.
A removal of partial dependence in the unnormalized relation CUSTOMER will produce two relations, ORDER and PRICE, which are in second normal form.
Example:

ORDER	(ORDER #	ITEM CODE	QUANTITY)
	1	A10	10
	1	C13	20
	2	A10	15
	2	B16	2
	3	B16	11

PRICE	(ITEM CODE	UNIT PRICE)
	A10	5
	C13	3
	B16	12

Update Problems with Unnormalized Relations   The following update problems are experienced in unnormalized relations:

- Insertion — if we wish to introduce a new item in the CUSTOMER relation with a specific UNIT PRICE, we cannot do so unless a customer places an order, since we need an ORDER #.
- Deletion — if the information about a customer order is deleted, the information about the item; e.g., UNIT PRICE, is also deleted.
- Modification — since the information about an item appears as many times as there are orders for it, modifications on the item information would be very difficult.

2.20.4   Third Normal Form

A normalized relation is said to be in third normal form if all its nonprime attributes are fully functionally and directly dependent on each candidate key.

Unnormalized Relation Example:

STOCK	(BIN #	PART #	QUANTITY	LEAD TIME	REORDER LEVEL)
	210	30	5	10	5
	211	30	10	10	5
	225	50	7	7	6
	231	81	3	15	10
	232	81	12	15	10

In the above relation we assume that a bin cannot hold stock of more than one part number (PART #). If BIN # is the candidate key, then the relation is not in third normal form, since the nonprime attributes LEAD TIME and RECORDER LEVEL are not directly dependent on BIN #.

Third Normal Form Example:

STOCK	(BIN #	PART #	QUANTITY)
	210	30	5
	211	30	10
	225	50	7
	231	81	3
	232	81	12

STOCK B	(PART #	LEAD TIME	REORDER LEVEL)
	30	10	5
	50	7	6
	81	15	10

2.21 Physical Database Design

This section discusses the objectives and approaches of physical design.

2.21.1 Objectives of Physical Database Design

The aim of physical database design is to produce a physical database which achieves the best performance at the least cost. The physical design process assumes that the logical design has been completed and that the logical schema presented is a true and complete representation of the real world. It also assumes that a database that follows the schema will be capable of supporting the user's needs.

2.21.2 Steps in the Physical Design Process

Physical database design can be broken into four main steps:

• Determining and documenting data representation
• Selecting and documenting access modes

- Allocating data to devices
- Loading and reorganizing the database

2.22   Determining Data Representation

Starting with the logical schema produced by logical data design, the physical designer must determine how each data element, record, and file is to be represented. For each element, the data type and size must be determined. The size and expected number of occurrences must be determined for each record.

Requirements for data types and size estimates may have been collected during the initial stage of logical design.

The physical designers can provide feedback to users and system developers concerning the storage implications of their database design.

2.23   Selecting the Access Methods

The selection of access methods depends on the organization's DBMS. However, in all cases the way in which each record type in the database will be accessed must be determined. Record types which will be directly accessible by their keys must be distinguished.

The access path; i.e., the sequence of records that must be retrieved to achieve a given process, must be described.

2.24   Allocating Data to Devices

Each record and file defined by the access method must be assigned to storage locations on physical devices. This assignment completes the physical design process. During this step, performance benefits can be gained by allocating the database to physical devices in a way that gives priority to frequently used data, or maximizes the likelihood that related data will be stored close together. This process is called clustering.

Clustering can take place at three levels:

- Records consisting of many attributes can be divided and subsets of the attribute stored together.
- Different records that are likely to be accessed simultaneously should be clustered together.

• Assign most frequently used portions of the database to a faster or more cost-effective storage medium.

2.25   Loading and Reorganizing the Database

In addition to developing the initial design, the physical designer is also responsible for seeing that the database is loaded properly and for any reorganization that may be required during the life of the database.

Reorganization of the database may imply changes in content, structure, access methods, or device allocation. Such changes may be required as a result of the introduction of new data elements or record types, as a result of new processing requirements, or simply to rectify the degradation in storage and processing efficiency.

2.26   Summary of Physical Database Design Processes

The implementation of databases from logical schemas requires the following selections:

• Types of logical relationships
• Access methods
• Secondary indices
• Types of pointers in relationship
• Allocation to storage devices
• Loading and reorganization of the database

3

Database Design Methodologies

This chapter presents an overview of database design and development methodologies and a detailed discussion of one of these methodologies — the entity-relationship (E-R) approach.

Database design refers to the process of arranging the data fields needed by one or more applications into an organized structure. That structure must foster the required relationships among the fields while conforming to the physical constraints of the particular database management system in use. There are really two parts to the process. There is logical database design, which is then followed by physical database design. (Logical database design is an implementation-independent exercise that is performed on the fields and relationships needed for one or more applications. Physical database design is an implementation-dependent exercise that takes the results of logical database design and further refines them according to the characteristics of the particular database management system in use.

A variety of reasons make careful database design essential. They include data redundancy, application performance, data independence, data security, and ease of programming. All are important factors in the data processing environment, and all can be adversely affected by a poor database design.

3.1   Review of Existing Methodologies

This action will present two of the most common database design methodologies. In the case of the first methodology, we will give only a brief introduction, whereas for the second we will give a more detailed discussion.

The first method, data normalization and data structuring, is representative of the class of methods that take as input a list of fields and the associations among those fields. The second method, the entity-relationship method, is representative of the class of methods that takes entities and relationships as input.

Database design using the entity-relationship model begins with a list of the entity types involved and the relationships among them. The philosophy of assuming that the designer knows what the entity types are at the outset is significantly different from the philosophy behind the normalization-based approach.

The entity-relationship approach uses entity-relationship diagrams, as illustrated in Figure 3-1. The rectangular boxes represent entity types, the diamond-shaped box represents a relationship between entities, and the circular figures represent attributes.

A more detailed discussion of the entity-relationship method is given in the following sections.

3.2   Detailed Discussion of Database Design

The process of developing a database structure from user requirements is called database design. Most practitioners agree that there are two separate phases to the database design process: the design of a logical database structure that is processable by the database management system (DBMS) and describes the user's view of data, and the selection of a physical structure, such as the indexed sequential or direct access method of the intended DBMS. Other than the logical/physical delineation, the overall structure of the design is not well-defined.

Novak and Fry defined four basic components that are necessary to achieve a database design methodology:

• A structured design process that consists of a series of steps where one alternative among many is chosen
• Design techniques to perform the enumeration required as stated previously, and evaluation criteria to select an alternative at each step

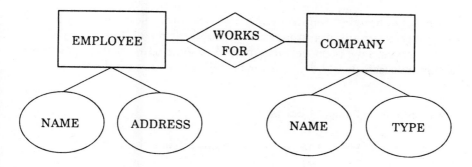

Figure 3-1   The Entity-Relationship Diagram

- Information requirements for input to the design process as a whole and to each step of the design process
- A descriptive mechanism to represent the information input and the results at each design step

Current database design technology shows many residual effects of its outgrowth from single-record file design methods. File design is primarily application-program dependent since the data has been defined and structured in terms of individual applications that use them. The advent of DBMS revised the emphasis in data and program design approaches. The concept of the integrated database spanning multiple users was a direct result of the complex data structuring capabilities which the DBMS afforded. Data can now be viewed as a corporate resource instead of as an adjunct to a program, and consequently should have an integrated requirements orientation instead of a single-program orientation.

Achieving a design which results in an acceptable level of database performance for all users has become a complex task. The database designer must be ever conscious of the cost/performance trade-offs associated with multiple users of a single integrated database. Potential savings of storage space and expanded applicability of databases into corporate decision making should be accompanied by a critical analysis of potential degradation of service to some users. Such degradation is to be avoided if possible. Acceptable performance for all users should be the goal.

Another aspect of database design is flexibility. Databases that are too tightly bound to current applications may have too limited a scope for many corporate enterprises.

Rapidly changing requirements and new data elements may result in costly program maintenance, a proliferation of temporary files, and increasingly poor performance. A meaningful overall database design process should account for both integration and flexibility.

3.2.1   Inputs to Design Process

The major classes of inputs to and results from the database design process are:

Inputs

• General information requirements
• Processing requirements
• DBMS specifications
• Operating system/hardware configuration
• Application program specifications

Results

• Logical database structure (user view)
• Storage structure (physical design)

The general information requirements represent various users' descriptions of the organization for which data are to be collected, the objectives of the database, and the users' views of which data should be collected and stored in the database. These requirements are considered to be process-independent because they are not tied to any specific database management system or application. Database design based on these requirements is considered to be advantageous for long-term databases that must be adaptable to changing processing requirements.

Processing requirements consists of three distinguishable components: specific data items required for each application, the data volume and expected growth, and processing frequencies in terms of the number of times each application must be run per unit time. Each of these components is very important to a particular stage or step of the database design process.

Performance measures and performance constraints are also imposed on the database design. Typical constraints include upper bounds on response times to queries, recovery times from system crashes, or specific data needed to support certain security or integrity requirements.

Specific performance measures used to evaluate the final structure might include update, storage, and reorganization costs in addition to response requirements.

The three major outputs of the database design process are the logical database structure, the physical storage structure, and specifications for application programs based on these database structures and processing requirements. As a whole, these results may be considered the specification for the final database implementation.

3.2.2 The Entity-Relationship (E-R) Approach Methodology

As more and more organizations implement systems employing database technology, the need for better methodologies to design these databases arises. The methodology described here provides a means of mapping the entity model produced from the data analysis phase to the database management system-supported structure.

The E-R approach requires several steps to produce a structure that is acceptable by the particular DBMS. These steps are:

• Data analysis
• Producing and optimizing the entity model
• Logical schema development
• Physical database design process

Definitions and Terminologies The following definitions and terminologies are frequently used in E-R theory and are basic to an understanding of the methodology. A more complete description of the process is available in existing literature.

1. An entity is a person, place, thing or concept that has characteristics of interest to the enterprise. An entity is something about which we store data. Examples of entities are: customer, part, employee, invoice, machine tool, salesperson, branch office, warehouse bin, shop order, shift report, product, product

description, ledger account, payment, debtor, and debtor analysis record. An entity has various attributes which we wish to record, such as color, size monetary value, percentage utilization, or name. For each entity type we have at least one record type. Sometimes more than one record type is used to store the data about the entity type. An entity type has one data item type or a group of data item types which uniquely identifies it. Entity is very often used interchangeably with entity type, entity instance, or entity class.

2. An attribute is a type of charactertistic property of an entity. It may be a data item which contains a single piece of information about an entity. Records are composed of attributes relating to a given entity. An attribute is often atomic; that is, it cannot be broken into parts that have meaning of their own. The term attribute is often used interchangeably with attribute type or attribute value. All attributes of a given type have the same format, interpretation, and range of acceptable values. An instance of a record has its own value of the attribute.

3. A relationship is a reason of relevance to the enterprise why entities from one or more entity types may be associated. It is a named connection between entity types that embodies some relevant information of value to an organization.

4. An access group is a group of data items or attributes which are always retrieved together because of common usage.

5. Access statistics are information collected about how often stored data is retrieved over a given period of time. Access statistics are used to determine where in a physical database the data will be stored.

3.2.3   The Data Analysis Phase

A fundamental part of the E-R methodology is the data analysis phase. This phase is concerned with identifying the data resources of an organization. Although methodologies for data analysis have stemmed from the need for a new approach to system design in a database environment, experience has shown that the concept of data analysis has a wider applicability, whether or not database software is involved. The approach to data analysis, the same scale involved, and the emphasis placed on the various tasks that must be done depend very much on the objectives of the project.

Davenport indicates that data analysis is used to:

- Determine the fundamental data resources of an organization
- Permit the design of flexible file structures capable of supporting a number of related applications
- Aid application development or conversion by providing a fundamental understanding of the data involved
- Form a basis for data control, security, and auditing of the resulting applications and systems
- Organize all relevant facts concerning the organization's data
- Aid the unification of an organization by indicating the commonality between its departments and data requirements
- Provide a basis for evaluating the structuring capability of competing database management systems

Further uses of data analysis are to:

- Identify the entities relevant to solve the existing data processing problem
- Determine the relationships among those entities
- Establish data and process definitions in a data dictionary
- Produce the entity model

The primary interest in data analysis tends to be to provide a sound basis for database design. It provides a disciplined approach toward cataloging the existing data in terms of the entities and relationships it represents. Without such an understanding of that part of the organization being analyzed, it is more difficult to establish whether and where a database could be efficiently installed. Data analysis provides a very effective means of communicating with non-data processing users, as it deals only with things that the users are familiar with and not with objects such as files and records.

The data analysis phase is sometimes referred to as requirements formulation and analysis, which involve the establishment of organization objectives, derivation of specific database requirements from these objectives or directly from management personnel, and documentation of these requirements in a form that is agreeable to management and database designers.

3.2.4   Conducting the Data Analysis Phase

Data analysis is best conducted by a team of individuals drawn from the user community, the systems development department, data administration group, and corporate standards department.

The data analysis team may not be involved in the requirement analysis phase of the project if that phase is limited to personal interviews with various levels of management and key employees involved in the processing of goods, services, and data in the organization. The result of such interviews should be flow diagrams of the process; e.g., illustrations of steps required to process an invoice and where in the organization these steps are undertaken, each employee who is involved, an identification of the data elements associated with each process, interfaces between processes, and a verification that both the interviewer and employee agree on the flow model semantics. Specific objectives and database requirements should be obtained at the highest possible level in the organization.

The data analysis team first identifies the entities needed to solve the problem defined by the users. During the initial stages of data analysis, all of the attributes of each entity may not be known. However, as each attribute is determined, the team should document the attribute definition and role in an appropriate data dictionary.

3.2.5   The Entity Model

During the data analysis phase, the major entities and their relationships are determined. These entities and their relationships are represented by models called entity models. The model is a diagrammatical representation of the relationship between the entity classes.

The representation allows us to include only those entities that are required to solve the particular data processing problem.

The entity model is essentially a real-world view of the organizational data in terms of the entities, attributes, and relationships.

During the entity modeling phase the most significant entity classes and relationships are defined. But inevitably a model will be revised, modified, or extended as a result of new knowledge about the entities being discovered. The model is used by the analysis team to:

- Reduce redundancy in the relationships
- Determine which entities are significant to the model and user requirement
- Resolve nonbinary relationships between entities

3.2.6 Approaches to Entity Model

There are two main approaches to entity modeling. These are:

- Top-down approach
- Bottom-up approach

The Top-down approach produces a global, corporate, or organizational view of the data before the application or user views are identified. The entities and relationships which are of interest to the organization are identified from the point of view of the organization and independent of any particular application.

The Bottom-up approach produces a composite or global view of the data based on the integration of several application views of the immediate problem requirements. The resulting model is limited to the immediate problem and cannot reflect the entire business activity of the corporation.

The Bottom-up approach is the one most often used in Entity Modelling. This approach produces a model with more clearly define boundaries than the Top-down approach. The processing requirements can be used by the analysis team to determine precisely what entities are required and the composition of those entities. The clustering of attributes into their respective entities or the splitting of entities can now be done with more precision. It is also easier to determine whether an attribute is indeed an attribute of an existing entity or is itself an entity with relationships to other entities when using this approach.

The Bottom-up approach produces entity models for each data area analyzed but these models can be merged together to produce an integrated model which will satisfy all data areas of the whole corporation. This integration phase initially involves some editing to remove inconsistencies in the type of attributes, entities or relationships. These inconsistencies may be in the form of one name referring to different components of the model (homonyms) or different name referring to the same component (synonyms).

3.2.7   Stages of Integration of Entity Models

The stages required to integrate entity models are as follows:

- identify any synonyms or homonyms in the different models. This task is made easier if a data dictionary is used. Components with homonyms will have to be renamed. Components with synonyms will have to be referred to by a single name.
- entity models for two data areas are integrated by super-imposing the identical or similar entity types in the different entity models. This may increase the total number of attributes in the entity type, as identical entity types in each model have been concerned with different subsets of the total group of properties.
- as a result of the integration, the composite entity model may contain redundant relationships. This redundant relationship may be eliminated. However, determining which relationships are directly significant and which are redundant can present difficulties which can only be solved by an understanding of the environment.

3.2.8   Entity Modeling Case Study

The following case study will serve to illustrate the use of entity modeling in database design. The database application is a general payroll system. The relevant department consists of a number of employees for whom paychecks must be processed. The employees' pensions can be paid in a lump sum or by installments upon retirement, death of employee, or resignation. The department also wishes to make inquiries about projects a particular employee has worked on.

The entities and relationships from the above case study are represented in the entity model (Figure 3-2).

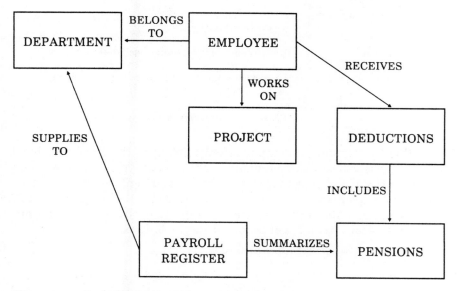

Figure 3-2   Entity Model for Paycheck Processing

The model shown in Figure 3-2 will require several revisions as the data analysis phase continues and the requirements are more clearly identified. Some researchers indicate that anywhere from 4 to 20 revisions to the model may be required. Revisions to the model may be required for any of the following reasons:

- one entity class may be shown to be a subset of another entity i.e., merging of entities
- and entity class may be best represented as a relationship between two entity classes
- some attributes of an existing entity may better describe a new entity i.e., splitting of entities
- the role of the attribute has changed during analysis
- more attributes are discovered during analysis

3.2.9   Application of Revisions to Entity Model

This section applies some of the above revision rules to Figure 3-1. Let us examine three of the entity classes of that Model.

Entity	Typical Attributes
Department	Department number, name, head, description
Employee	Employee social security number, name, address, status, supervisor
Pensions	Pensions identifier, type, description, amount

In the department and employee entity classes, the attributes head and supervisor best describe another entity class. We can now create a new entity class, manager, for example, and replace the two attributes with pointers or relationship codes to the original entity classes. We can also add new attributes to the entity class, manager. Some typical attributes of manager are as follows:

Entity	Typical Attributes
Manager	Manager identifier, description, authority

This revision to the model will also require that we establish two more relationships; i.e., manager/department and manager/employee relationships.

In the pensions entity class the attribute "type" indicates that pensions can be paid upon retirement, death of employee, resignation of employee, in a lump sum, annually or via deferred payment.

Depending on the queries the users want to make, one may decide to split the pensions entity class into one or more entities. For example, we may have one entity class for natural retirements and another for all lump sum payments. In this case, the entities are application views of the entity class pensions. We will discuss application views in a later section.

In summarizing revisions to the entity model, we may list a few rules in determining when an attribute of an entity is best treated as an entity in its own right related to the first entity. The rules are:

• Determine if the attribute itself has any other related attributes
• Determine if the new entity is required in order to solve the data processing problem
• Determine if the attribute in fact identifies the second entity
• Determine if the new entity is related to the original entity
• Determine if the new entity is related to any other entities in the model

3.3   Deriving Entity Models from Traditional or Flat Files

This section discusses some approaches for deriving entity models from flat files or databases that were not designed using E-R methodology. There are no hard and fast rules for this derivation. One would have liked to say that there is a one-to-one correspondence between the entity classes in a model and the number of files/descriptions (FD) in a program. However, the clustering of data items from which the logical files were constructed may not be the same clustering required for the respective entity classes. Nevertheless, the following simple rules can be followed when converting from flat files to the entity model of that application:

- List all the file types in the relevant programs
- List all the logical records in the files
- List all the data items in the records
- Eliminate redundancies and inconsistencies in the data items and logical records
- List all possible combinations of entity classes from the logical records. The record name is an indicator of the entity class.
- List all codes in the records that can give the relationships of the entity model
- Conduct a preliminary data analysis of the data items
- Cluster the attributes into their respective entity classes

This procedure will result in a baseline entity model which will serve as a framework for making further revisions necessary due to more detailed data analysis.

The procedure to follow for old databases created by methods other than E-R methodology will depend largely on how the data was physically clustered for data retrieval. Very often, if the physical clustering was performance-oriented, the logical clustering into entity classes becomes a very complex, if not impossible, task.

It is my experience that the most productive method is still to obtain data definitions for all the data items in the databases, take the applications that use those data items, and cluster the data items into entity classes using any known data analysis techniques.

The entity model for the particular user area can then be obtained by an integration or superimposition of the individual program-oriented models.

3.3.1   Superimposition of Entity Models

In the conversion of existing physical databases back to their entity model equivalents, the designer may arrive at several different models depending on the programs or applications from which the models were derived. He or she should then attempt to remove redundancies and inconsistencies by superimposing the models from several programs to arrive at one integrated model.

The superimposition of entity models would allow the designer to determine:

- The common entity classes and attributes. These can be recognized on the basis of names only.
- The inconsistencies in the naming and use of attributes. These inconsistencies exist when two entities with different names are clearly shown to be one and the same entity.
- The adequacy of the model in terms of meeting the needs of the user.
- Whether attributes clustered into an entity class are indeed members of another entity class or new entity classes themselves.
- The existence of inconsistencies in the relationships.

The superimposed entity model can now be used as a framework for further revisions to arrive at an integrated entity model that will serve a larger data area than several smaller application-oriented models.

3.3.2   Clustering of Entity Classes

Clustering of entity classes in database design may occur in the logical or physical design stage. In the physical design stage, the clustering of the entity classes may be done solely on the basis of performance considerations.

The entity classes may be merged or split into different physical databases depending upon the access requirements.

The logical clustering of entity classes is dependent upon the inherent nature of the data and data structure, whereas physical clustering is not. It is a necessary but not sufficient rule to say that attributes are clustered within an entity class because they best identify and describe that entity class, and entity classes are clustered into an entity model to satisfy a user's data processing requirement.

The logical clustering of entity classes is done to satisfy the following:

- The area served by the data or from which the data originated
- The inherent data structure
- The local view of the user
- The usage of the data
- The queries against the data
- The data processing needs of the user

The clustering of entity classes on the basis of data area is essentially that all data for which the accounting department has a functional responsibility will be clustered as accounting data. Similarly, all data for which the personnel department has that responsibility will be clustered as personnel data. The data areas are usually determined by the same methods used to create the organizational structure or boundaries.

The inherent data structure of an organization would indicate that employees are assigned to departments, assigned to projects; customers place orders; and orders are for products. Thus, in clustering of entity classes, the cluster must reflect that inherent data structure. The inherent data structure now reflects the business practices of the organizations and the clustering would also reflect those practices.

The clustering of entity classes on the basis of the local view of the user can be translated to mean that only those entities in which the user has some interest are assembled. The cluster may be part of a larger cluster or an amalgamation of several clusters. Thus, if the user wanted to determine the projects an employee worked on, his local views would consist of the cluster of the employee and project entity classes.

The attributes within an entity class and the clustering of the entity classes must satisfy the queries made against them. For example, one could not satisfy a query about an employee's skill and education if these attributes are not in the entity class. Similarly, a query about the percentage of an employee's time spent on a project could not be answered if there was not a clustering of employee and project entity classes.

As in entity modeling, so in clustering of entity classes the object of the exercise is to satisfy the data processing need of the user. The adequacy of the model is measured in relation to how well those needs are met. The entity classes will be clustered in accordance with those needs.

3.3.3   Application View and Logical Schema Design

An application view may be defined as the set of data required by that particular application to fulfill a specific data processing need. For example, one application may be interested in materializing employee name and social insurance number as its employee entity class, while another may materialize employee name, social insurance number, and salary as its employee entity class. In turn, these two entity classes may be just a subset of a larger set of attributes, which make up a corporate or global entity class called employee entity class.

We may have application views of:

• An entity class
• Cluster of entity classes
• Cluster of entity classes and physical databases
• Cluster of physical databases

The logical schema may be defined as the mapping of the entity model into the constructs provided by the database management system (DBMS), for example, the mapping of the entity model into an IMS construct. In general, the logical schema indicates how the model will be stored and accessed. In the design of the logical schema, some restructuring of the model and changes to conform to the DBMS may be necessary.

The entity model is not the logical schema. The entity model is:

• A representation of real-world view of the data
• The building blocks used for further data analysis and database design
• Not restricted to any database management systems (DBMS)
• Not directly implementable
• A stable framework or frame of reference into which new entities, attributes, and relationships can fit as more organizational database needs evolve

3.3.4   Logical Schema—Case Study

In this section, I will endeavor to construct a logical schema from the entity model shown in Figure 3-2. Due to space limitations, I will not

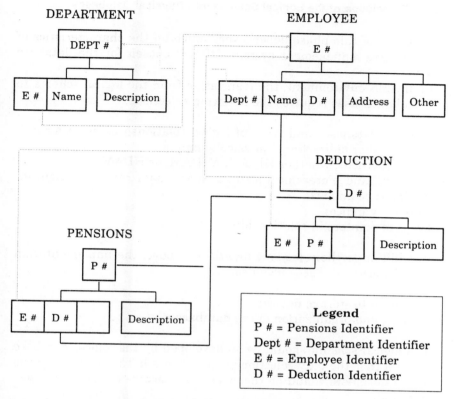

Figure 3-3   Logical Schema for Paycheck Entity Model

do the schema for the entire model as shown. A partial logical schema is shown below.

In the logical schema of Figure 3-3, we should note that the hierarchical data structure of IMS is now applied to the entity model. We also see that the pointers and unique keys are also imposed on the entity model.

If other relationships than those shown in the logical schema are required, these are shown including all materialized attributes of relationships and their pointers. The logical schema should also show the occurrences of major groups of data or segments.

It should be noted that the logical schema for relational and network databases will exhibit the constructs provided by their respective database management system.

3.3.5   Translation of the Logical Schema into Physical Databases

The details of this phase depend very much on the characteristics of the database management system (DBMS) chosen for the database design.

In an IMS environment, the translation from the logical schema to physical databases requires the following selections:

- Physical databases and types of logical relationships, whether unidirectional or bidirectional physically paired
- Access methods, whether HISAM, MIDAM, or HDAM
- Segments and hierarchical structures and data representation, including type and size
- Secondary indices
- Types of pointers in relationship

In addition to the selections mentioned above, the implementation of the physical databases includes:

- Allocation to storage devices
- Loading and organization of the databases

The logical schema should be so developed by the logical database designers that the only selection requirements left to be done by the physical designers would be the selection of access methods and secondary indices.

The translation of logical schemas into physical databases is dealt with at considerable length in the current literature.

Finally, Hubbard indicates that the following rules should be followed during the physical design process:

- Each entity class should be treated as a physical database.
- If two entity classes share a relationship between at least one attribute and the primary key, then the structures should consist of two physical databases with physical or virtual pairing between them.
- Parent-child relationship should be defined in a single physical database.
- Frequently accessed segments should be kept as close to their root as possible.

- Reduce the time for searching large data groups by using secondary indexing.
- Segments of varying sizes should not be placed in the same data set group if frequent inserts or deletes are to be performed.

3.4 Summary

This chapter has served to discuss database design methodologies in general and the entity-relationship (E-R) approach methodology in particular.

The chapter started off with a review of the existing methodologies and highlighted two methodologies. These were (a) data normalization and data structuring and (b) entity-relationship.

The chapter gave a step-by-step approach to design using the E-R method and cited a case study using a payroll application.

Chapter

4

Database Security, Privacy, and Integrity

Data security is defined as the procedural and technical measures required to:

- Prevent any deliberate denial of service
- Prevent unauthorized access, modification, use, and dissemination of data stored or processed in a computer system
- Protect the system in its integrity from physical harm

The access control requirements are particularly important in time-shared and multiprogrammed systems in which multiple users must be prevented from interfering with each other, and users must be prevented from gaining unauthorized access to each other's data or programs.

Privacy is an issue that concerns the computer community with maintaining personal information on individual citizens in computerized record-keeping systems. It deals with the right of the individual regarding the collection of information in a record-keeping system about his person and activities and the processing, dissemination, storage, and use of this information in making determinations about him.

Integrity is a measure of the quality and reliability of the data on which computer-based information systems depend. Many computerized databases in use today suffer from high error rates in the data they receive and are consequently riddled with bad data. With incorrect data, even the most efficient and sophisticated system is almost useless.

Computer privacy is concerned with the moral and legal requirements to protect data from unauthorized access and dissemination. The issues involved in computer privacy are therefore political decisions regarding who may have access to what and who may disseminate what, whereas the issues involved in computer security are procedures and safeguards for enforcing the privacy decisions.

Privacy issues affect all aspects of computer security because of legislative measures enacted. With due consideration of its social implications, legislation for computer privacy determines the type of information collected and by whom, the type of access and dissemination, the subject rights, the penalties, and the licensing matter.

In 1973 the Department of Health, Education, and Welfare proposed several actions to be taken to help protect individual privacy. This report proposed the following fundamental principles of fair information practice to guide the development of regulations and laws concerning privacy.

- There must be no personal-data record-keeping systems whose very existence is secret.
- There must be a way for an individual to find out what information about him is in a record, and how it is used.
- There must be a way for an individual to prevent information about him obtained for one purpose from being used or made available without his consent.
- There must be a way for an individual to correct or amend a record of identifiable information about him.
- Any organization creating, maintaining, using, or disseminating records of identifiable personal data must assure the reliability of the data for their intended use and must take reasonable precautions to prevent misuse of the data.

Guidelines and procedures may be established for accountability, levels of control, type of control, rules, and checklists. Preventive measures and recovery due to internal threats and external intrusions are also a part of data security. For these threats and intrusions, the causes, effects, and means must be studied. More difficult aspects of data security research include risk analysis, threat analysis, assessment, and insurance. By knowing the risks involved, data security may be expressed in terms of quantitative indicators, cost factors, and options. These discussions are included in the remaining sections of this chapter.

4.1 Conducting a Threat Analysis

A threat is defined as that which has the potential to menace, abuse, or harm. A threat can either modify or destroy the functional purpose of an object, and hence is a source of potential danger. In the context of our discussion of threat analysis and data security, we shall express a threat as the danger to which the data is exposed.

A threat analysis is defined as the methodology employed to assess the level of the system's security and the protection mechanisms in place to counter the threat. Threat analysis is also useful in designing cost-effective security systems.

A good threat analysis is an important element in the review of security needs. Together with an analysis of vulnerability, it provides the basic data needed to assess the risks. Even if threats are not expressed in probabilistic terms, their existence should be recognized and priority ratings should be assigned.

The threats considered in this chapter will be limited to those faced by the data. We will not consider those threats to physical security usually countered by the installation of some physical measures. In this category of threats are fire hazards, illegal entry into a specific computer installation, and hardware failure.

The methodology most frequently employed in the studies that produced most of the data for this chapter is the checklist method. This approach consists essentially of a series of questions asked to determine what protection measures are in place to counter threats against specific objects.

Considerable attention should be devoted to planning the questionnaire and the follow-up interviews with respondents. The researcher should set specific objectives and have clearly measurable goals for each associated task. The scheduling and coordinating of interviews with the various respondents should also receive considerable attention.

4.1.1 Threat Analysis Case Study

The threat analysis detailed in this section was conducted in a database environment using IMS as the database management system (DBMS). The objects selected for the study included:

- Program specification blocks (PSB) library
- Database description (DBD) library
- Application control block (ACB) library
- Data dictionary
- Source and object modules for Cobol, Mark IV, and application development facility (ADF)
- Cobol message processing programs (MPP)
- Data files

The primary goal of the questionnaire was to determine what protection existed to counter the following categories of threats:

- Unauthorized access to the library
- Unauthorized manipulation of the members of the library
- Authorized users browsing the library
- Unauthorized use of utility routines
- Inadequate auditing and monitoring of threats
- Obtaining access to the database by bypassing the PSB library
- Illegal use of processing options
- Destruction of the storage medium
- Unauthorized distribution or exposure
- Unauthorized copying or altering of the libraries
- Illegal deletion of stored data
- Passing of sensitive data by authorized users to unauthorized users
- Unauthorized copying or altering of the library
- Access to residues of data
- Unauthorized use of terminals
- Collusion of employees
- Denial of access to system resources
- Inadequate documentation and historical change data to establish audit trails
- One programmer having sole knowledge of access to and maintenance responsibility for sensitive programs
- Inadequate training and attitude toward data security
- Exposure of sensitive data following abnormal ending of job

An example of a typical question found on the questionnaire is: Does the computer give a dump of memory if an abnormal end of job occurs during the running of a sensitive program?

The response to the several questionnaires are then analyzed to determine the level of protection available to each specific object.

4.1.2   Analysis of Results

The results obtained form the responses to the questionnaire agreed favorably with results from similar surveys. They indicated that the following threats existed:

* Inadequate authentication of user identification
* Inadequate controls over the use of utilities and special purpose programs
* Inability to identify terminals and users in the event of a breach of security
* Need for risk assessment

Some of the major systems surveyed required identification for access to data that depended on personal knowledge of corporate structure, manager's position code, or manager's signing authority, and, in general, on information that can easily be obtained by corporate customers. The ease with which such information could be obtained presented considerable security problems.

In view of the ease of obtaining such information, the authentication process should be stringent enough to provide some protection for the passwords, user identification, or sign-on identification. The authentication process should not be based on further personal knowledge of the authorized user. For example, requiring a user to give the birth date, name of first child, or high school attended as authentication for an already weakened identification scheme only serves to further weaken the system. The unauthorized user armed with such easily obtainable knowledge will be in a position to pass the authentication requirements with little difficulty.

It has been demonstrated that it is possible for an authorized user to retrieve a user's source program and alter the code without detection. The unauthorized user could illegally embed statements in the user's code, recompile the code, and return the object code to the load library. Existing controls did not restrict by, for example, a user profile giving access to user's source libraries by other users. A user profile would restrict that user to certain libraries, programs, or portions of stored data.

In a similar manner, control should exist over certain specialized routines, utility programs, and programs that allow specially trained programmers to bypass standard procedures to gain access to stored data. Administrative controls should be in place which outline what procedures one should follow to gain access to routines and utilities. These controls should include who can authorize use of such programs, signatures required, logs to be completed, and any follow-up reporting that should be done.

The responses to the survey showed that there was almost no ability to make a positive identification of a terminal or its user in the event of a security breach. The failure was due to the following:

• Inadequate authentication
• Use of logical terminal identifications
• Inadequate audit trails

The protection mechanism to counter this threat should include restricting the use of certain terminals to certain types of transactions, allowing certain terminals to process during certain periods, and include in the authentication process certain transformations that require keys that would link the terminal to the corresponding identity.

Finally, the analysis of the responses reveal that consideration should be given to some or all of the following protection mechanisms:

• Frequent changing password
• Levels of authority and processing functions
• Sign off automatically after a period of inactivity
• Fixed time to bring up terminals and period processing
• Online auditing — one terminal used to maintain monitoring and surveillance
• Dedicated telephone lines
• Encryption of files
• Administrative control of utilities
• Erasure of residues on tapes/disks
• Log of all terminal users

- Hardwired terminals for entering specific transactions
- Individual libraries — users are restricted by either password or user identification to libraries for which they have authorization

4.1.3 Conducting a Risk Assessment

In addition to conducting a threat analysis, another useful exercise in implementing security safeguards in an organization is conducting a risk assessment.

A risk assessment is an analytical process designed to quantify the data security required by an organization. It considers the threats to data and the loss that would occur if a threat were to materialize. The purpose of a risk assessment is to help an organization establish priorities for cost-effective safeguards to reduce the probability of given threats or aid in recovery from a loss.

For some potential threats, a risk assessment may show the potential loss to be catastrophic to the organization. In some cases, when a security breach can be evaluated in terms of cost, delay, disclosure, or other measure, establishing a base level of security may be a desirable first step.

The risk analysis provides a rational approach toward choosing security safeguards. A security program should logically provide protection in the most economical manner.

The following questions, therefore, should be answered in the course of a risk assessment:

- What are the specific results desired; that is, exactly how much security is required?
- What is the proper balance between security program cost and potential benefits?
- When trade-offs can be made between protection and recovery, how much effort should be expended on each?

Several full-length checklists and questionnaires for conducting risk assessment are available in current literature on the subject. The author developed a questionnaire as part of the database security research conducted during the past five years. This questionnaire is illustrated as EXHIBIT A.

EXHIBIT A

USER RISK ANALYSIS

FOR

_____ SYSTEM

PREPARED BY _____

ORIGIN DATE _____

1. Uses of the Application Output (LIST)

    A. _____

    B. _____

    C. _____

    D. _____

2. Dependencies
    Are there other uses of the Application Output outside of your specific area? Please list.

USE	USER
_____	_____
_____	_____
_____	_____

3. Critical Dates or Time Periods
    Please list any critical dates or time periods (e.g., fiscal year end, Christmas checks).

Date	Reason	Brief Description
OF: _____		Criticality

4. Dollar Risk vs. Application Outage Duration
    Please complete Table 1 (attached).

5. Critical Files

    A. Please list critical files

    _____

    _____

    _____

    _____

    B. File backup requirements

    Are the files backed up by EDP resource?   _____
    If so, how often?   _____
    How are the files backed up?
    a) Magnetic tape in vault   _____
    b) Microfilm   _____
    c) If microfilm, where stored?   _____
    d) Estimate time to recover if microfilm
        or
        listing is only backed up partially?   _____
    e) If backup is by microfilm, how often
        is it updated?   _____

6. Revenue Estimate

    Revenue earned is _____ per _____.

7. Fallback Model

    A. Is a manual fallback system feasible?
        a) If so, how long to put it in place?   _____
        b) Cost to put it in place?   _____
        c) Estimated running cost of manual
            system is _____ per _____.

B. Time frame when manual fallback system
ceases to be feasible? _____

C. Estimated loss as a result of interruption.
Please complete Table 2.

8. Remote Access System Data
Is the application run remotely from the
computer center?
If yes, _____

A. What type of terminal is used? _____

B. Is your terminal connected to the computer via:
a) leased lines?
b) dial up plus acoustic coupler?
c) other (state)?

_____

_____

C. Is your terminal in the same building as
the computer? _____

D. Do you use a password to sign in on the system?
If so,
a) Who determines the password
(user/technical branch)?
b) How? _____
c) How often will passwords be changed
and by whom? _____
d) Would you change the password when
an employee who knows the password
terminates his/her employment? _____
e) How many people know the password? _____

E. Would you consider the information transmitted/received over the terminal

   a) Business confidential?   _____

   b) Personally private?   _____

   c) Information whose dissemination
      should be controlled?   _____

   d) Used in making management decisions? _____

   e) Information that may be disseminated
      to anyone within a department without
      control?   _____

F. Do you employ any cryptographic methods to protect vital data? If so,

   a) Are software or programmatic techniques
      used?   _____

   b) Are hardware devices used?   _____
      If so, name the manufacturer and model number

      _____

   c) The cryptographic methods are used because of:
      i) pertinent legislation; ii) user priorities; iii) other

G. What programming language can you utilize from your terminal? Please list and encircle those not required

      _____

H. Which of the following security measures pertaining to terminals have you considered adequate for your needs?

   a) Nondisplay screen mode for entering the sign-on
      parameters and update passwords.

   b) The defined terminal access be restricted to time of
      day?

   c) The defined terminal to be automatically signed off
      after extended periods of inactivity?

d) In the case of attempted violations, the system iden-
    tifies the responsible terminal/user?

e) The transaction can be entered only from the termi-
    nals so authorized?

I. Security audit report(s):
    Please indicate reports applicable to this application:
    a) RACF
    b) Access matrix model
    c) Generated from DBMS log tapes
    d) Security audit trail

J. Other potential problem areas not covered above

Table 1   Risk (in Dollars) vs. EDP Application Outage Duration

Outage Duration	Dollar Risk	Reason For Risk	Time *	Cost	Remarks
1 Day					
2 Days					
3 Days					
4 Days					
5 Days					
6 Days					
7 Days					
2 Weeks					
3 Weeks					
4 Weeks					
2 Months					
3 Months					

* Time when you would start manual.

Table 2   Estimated Business Lost (Revenue) as a Result of Interrupted or Degraded Service

Duration	Revenue Lost (%)	Revenue Lost ($)	Critical Time *	Remarks
1 Day				
2 Days				
3 Days				
4 Days				
5 Days				
6 Days				
7 Days				
2 Weeks				
3 Weeks				
4 Weeks				
2 Months				
3 Months				

* Duration of interruptions or degradation.

4.1.4   Achieving Database Privacy

Privacy of information in a database is lost either by accident or deliberately induced disclosure. The most common causes of accidental disclosures are failures of hardware and use of partially debugged programs. Improvements in hardware reliability and various memory protection schemes have been suggested as countermeasures. Deliberate efforts to infiltrate an online database can be classified as either passive or active.

Passive infiltration may be accomplished by electromagnetic pickup of the traffic at any point on the system.

Active infiltration — an attempt to enter the database to directly obtain or alter information — can be overtly accomplished through normal access procedures by:

• Using legitimate access to the database to ask unauthorized questions or to browse in unauthorized data
• Masquerading as a legitimate user after having obtained proper identification by other means
• Having access to the database by virtue of your position

The above spectrum of threats can be countered by a number of techniques and procedures. Some of them were originally introduced into time-shared, multiuser systems to prevent users from inadvertently disturbing each other's programs, and then expanded to protect against accidental or deliberately induced disclosures of data. In the following discussion, we cite some of these countermeasures.

4.1.5   Access Management

These techniques are aimed at preventing unauthorized users from obtaining services from the system or gaining access to its files. The procedures involved are authorization, identification, and authentication. Authorization is given for certain users to enter the database and request certain types of information. Any user attempting to enter the system must first identify himself and his location, and then authenticate his identification.

4.1.6   Privacy Transformations

Privacy transformations are techniques for coding the data in user-processor communications or in files to conceal information. Privacy transformations consist of sets of logical operations on the individual characters of the data.

Privacy transformations break down into two general types: irreversible and reversible. Irreversible includes aggregation and random modification. In this case, valid statistics can be obtained from such data, but individual values cannot be obtained. Reversible privacy transformations are as follows:

- Coding — a word in one language replaces a group of words in another
- Compression — remove redundancies and blanks from transmitted data
- Substitution — letters from one or more items are replaced
- Transposition — all the letters in the clear text appear in the ciphered text, but in a distorted sequence
- Composite transformation — combinations of the above methods

4.1.7   Cryptographic Controls and Data Transformation

Cryptographic transformations were recognized long ago to be an effective protection mechanism in communication systems. In the past, they have been used mainly to protect information transferred through communication lines.

There is still much debate as to the cost/benefit of encrypting large production databases. The author's experience with encryption indicates that because of the need to produce clear text from large encrypted databases, the cost of this type of control makes it prohibitive.

4.1.8   Database Integrity

A database integrity system is used to prevent certain types of inconsistencies introduced by errors of the users or their application programs from affecting the contents of the database. By enforcing semantic restrictions on the information, it is possible to ensure that the contents of the database is correct and that no inconsistencies exist between related information. The increased use of data dictionaries has gone a long way in ensuring integrity of databases.

The data dictionary documents what validity and edit rules are to be applied to the data. These rules can be classified into a few basic categories, which correspond to specifications of range, sets of values permitted, format, uniqueness of some values, nonmissing values for a field, and interfield assertions.

Systems surveillance, measurement, and auditing are critical elements in providing the technical base for adequate integrity.

The effectiveness and operability of the entire system, especially the protection mechanisms, must be continually scrutinized and measured. Management must also be able to detect and to respond to events that constitute system security threats.

Finally, the introduction of a properly functioning audit system should allow the internal auditors to indicate that the occurrence of certain events should trigger audit trails that cannot be destroyed deliberately.

5

Development of Security Controls

This chapter discusses some features of database security, privacy, and integrity beyond a level that may be considered introductory. The features are termed advanced because they are features a worker wishing to install security mechanisms in his organization may select for direct implementation. The chapter does not give a step-by-step approach to the implementation of these features but discusses the issues a security analyst must consider when deciding to implement security measures.

The chapter starts off by discussing top-level management involvement in database security, privacy, and integrity. The author has discovered that one of the main causes of inadequate database protection or no protection in several organizations is due to the fact that top-level management does not see the need to incur the cost of protecting database contents. The analyst who wants to pursue the installation of security measures at his installation must first convince management of the need for security and get their support, not only during the implementation of the measures but for constant monitoring of the performance and adequacy of the measures and the upgrading of those measures as warranted.

In order to determine the adequacy of existing security measures, the level of protection required for the database content, and the cost to install these measures, the analyst must conduct a risk analysis.

The risk analysis and the need for risk analysis is discussed in later sections of the chapter.

The chapter concludes by discussing some protection mechanisms that may be implemented by organizations to achieve data security.

Protection mechanisms may be defined as the controls implemented by the organization to achieve data security and protection. The mechanisms discussed in this chapter can be divided into two categories: mechanisms or controls that are implemented external to the computer system and operating software and those implemented as part of the operating or management systems software. Administrative controls would fall into the category of external protection mechanisms, whereas the following controls could be considered as internal protection mechanisms:

- Auditing and monitoring the database
- Authorization schemas such as in access control matrix
- Resource access control facility (RACF)

5.1   Top-Level Management Involvement in Database Security, Privacy, and Integrity

My four years of research in database security, privacy, and integrity revealed that one of the major reasons for the noneffort or failure of database security efforts in most corporations is the lack of involvement and support by the top-level management.

We would have assumed, with the overwhelming statistics relative to the ease with which computer systems are penetrated and the resulting loss, that management will support a program to provide adequate security. But this assumption is not necessarily valid.

For one thing, most managers are inundated with immediate problems. The one thing they feel they do not need is to be further burdened with hypothetical problems. But security deals with hypothetical problems; i.e., things that might happen.

Further, these are things that management hopes will not happen. They involve "bad" human behavior, in most cases, while managers prefer to deal with "good" behavior, such as how employees can get their work done more efficiently, get company problems solved, and increase company profits.

The net result, as one might expect, is that security considerations tend to be postponed. They are postponed, that is, until some serious consequence occurs from a breach of security. Then there may be a flurry of excitement, as an attempt is made to bolster security measures.

As I see it, management's willingness to consider the security problem is the most important single factor in the whole security program.

For one thing, management makes the critical decision at the outset as to whether the security problem will be approached. They must set the policies, ground rules, and scope of the security project. They create the reviews to determine whether things have changed to the point where major new protective measures must be considered.

Management sets the guidelines and procedures for an effective system of internal controls. These controls deal with handling the assets and liabilities of the organization. They identify the sensitive data and programs that need to be protected. They classify and itemize their existence, importance, or need for protection.

Further, these assets and liabilities can be protected, in part, by protecting information about them. For example, if a fictitious payment transaction is entered into the accounts receivable database, an asset is lost. Also if a fictitious invoice is entered into the accounts payable database and is paid, an asset is lost. If a manipulated transaction causes a valuable piece of property, a vehicle, or piece of equipment to be written off as salvage and is taken by some unauthorized personnel, an asset is lost. Protection against these threats is accomplished by controls set up by management that make it difficult to enter such fictitious transactions into the system. Management support for a security program may be in any of the following forms:

• Assignment of major responsibilities for the program
• Organization and assignment of the team for the security program
• Setting policies and general control objectives
• Undertaking a cost/benefit study to determine what protection features to implement

Management can set the desired tone for the whole security program by identifying those general control standards that it wishes to emphasize by the following means:

• Study the existing protection to point out where additional or improved protection is needed
• Design and install the needed protection, under the responsibility of operating management
• Check the effectiveness of the whole internal protection system by means of periodic audits

5.2   Administrative Controls

Administrative controls may be defined as management policies formulated to ensure adequate maintenance of a selective access program, whether it be selective authorization to data files or physical areas. They may include the development and implementation of security policies, guidelines, standards, and procedures.

Effective administrative controls can go a long way in helping to ensure that an organization has a secure operating database environment. These controls will certainly assist in reducing or eliminating both deliberate and accidental threats. Once an intruder realizes that his chances of being detected are good, he may be deterred from attempting to breach the security. This determination of his probability of being detected can be made from his knowledge of the existing administrative controls. For example, if the intruder knows that there is a requirement for the user's name and terminal log on times to be recorded, then he will very likely not use the terminal.

The probability of accidental threats succeeding decreases with an increase in the user's knowledge of the operating environment and requirements. Clear and precise administrative procedures and assertions help to increase that knowledge and, in turn, decrease the probability of successful accidental threats.

Administrative controls, and security features in particular, should be developed in parallel with the actual systems and programs development. A group consisting of internal auditors, development team, and users should be assigned to develop these controls and standards.

Administrative controls can be defined in the following areas:

- Top-level management decisions — decisions pertaining to the selection and evaluation of safeguards
- Security risk assessment studies — identify and rank the events that would compromise the security of the database and the information stored in it
- Personnel management — pertain to employee hiring and firing procedures, employee rules of conduct and enforcement
- Data handling techniques — a well-defined set of rules describing the precautions to be used and the obligations of personnel during the handling of all data
- Data processing practices — include the methods to control accountability for data, verification of the accuracy of data, inventories of storage media

- Programming practices — pertain to the discipline employed in the specification, design, implementation, programming, coding, and debugging of the system
- Assignment of responsibilities — assign each individual a specific set of responsibilities toward carrying out certain security functions for which he is held responsible
- Procedures auditing — an independent examination of established security procedures to determine their ongoing effectiveness

5.3 Auditing and Monitoring the Database

Auditing and monitoring are integral features of database security. Should a violation be attempted, the system must be able to detect it and react effectively to it. Detection then implies that the system has a threat-monitoring capability. Threat monitoring requires the following actions:

- Monitoring the events of the system as related to security
- Recognizing a potential compromise to the security system
- Diagnosing the nature of the threat
- Performing compensatory actions
- Reporting the event
- Recording the event

While threat monitoring is an active form of surveillance, an equally important but more passive form is auditability of the database. A security audit should be able to cover the past events of the system and, in particular, cover all security-related transactions.

Audit trails that can lead to the identity of users, terminals, and authorizing bodies should be a feature of all applications.

The monitoring process within an organization should include the ability to determine whether:

- The controls over the database administration function are effective
- The process by which sensitive data is determined is adequate
- The procedures by which security violations are detected are in place and effective
- The extent to which data access is restricted to only authorized individuals is workable

- The ability exists to restrict access by a program to data, other programs, and libraries
- Terminal security features such as log on, log off, and restart are adequate and effective
- The procedures to follow during processing interruptions are effective

The importance of keeping records and logs of events affecting the database and its environment cannot be overemphasized. The events recorded should include performance data, all error or abnormal events, all transactions related to sensitive information, and all overrides of established system's controls.

Several database management systems provide logging capabilities as part of their package. These logs should be investigated for their adequacy and ability to meet the auditing requirements of the environment. Organizations should not be hesitant to design and implement their own in-house logging facilities if the manufacturer's prove inadequate.

Any security effort in an organization should eventually involve internal auditors. This involvement becomes mandatory because of the changing requirements for evaluating and verifying controls in a secure database environment.

Personnel responsible for security can offer considerable assistance to the auditors in determining the accuracy, integrity, and completeness of systems.

Researchers are now suggesting that the internal auditors become involved in the development stages of a system and not only in the postinstallation evaluation. The auditors' experience should provide the development teams with an insight into the various methods they can use to approach their responsibilities in controlling and auditing the total information-processing system.

Because of the rapidly changing database technology, internal auditors need to constantly upgrade their skills. System development teams with current knowledge should assist the auditors in filling the gaps in their knowledge of techniques and concepts of integrated database system design.

The development teams should strive to increase management's awareness of changes in the data processing environment as they affect internal audit and the controls governing data processing.

Finally, the following list of management activities should enhance the internal auditing capabilities within a corporation and especially as they affect the database environment:

- Ensure that all staff realize the importance of internal auditing in the security effort
- Issue a clearly defined internal audit mandate that specifies the responsibility of internal audit as it relates to all phases of the security effort
- Clearly define the working relationship among users, internal auditors, and development teams responsible for database security, privacy, and integrity
- Encourage the development of new techniques and internal audit approaches to ensure the security, privacy, and integrity of the database
- Require the development of security control guidelines
- Ensure that internal auditors participate in the security effort

5.4   Types of Protection Mechanism

In an earlier section, I introduced two classes of protection mechanisms: those built into the computer operating system (internal mechanisms) and those not linked to the operating system (external mechanisms). The next few sections discuss some of those protection mechanisms in more detail.

5.4.1   The Access Matrix as a Protection Mechanism

The access matrix is an internal protection mechanism built into the operating system. It is essentially a set of tables that indicate who has access to what data. The access matrix consists of the following components:

- Objects to be protected
- Subjects seeking access to these objects
- Different protection levels for each object
- Rules that determine how the subjects access each object
- A monitor that mediates all access of a subject to an object
- Directories containing information about the objects and subjects. The information on the object consists of such things as the unique identifier, protection level, types of access permitted, and data types. The information on the subject consists of the unique identifier and class of subjects.

The interaction between the subjects and objects can be represented by an access control matrix (see Figure 5-1). The protectable objects are the row-components of the matrix. The subjects seeking access to the objects are the column-components of the matrix. Each entry in the access matrix determines the access rights of the subject to the object and is defined as the access attribute in the model.

The access matrix model is dynamic enough to include any class of objects or subjects within the data processing environment. It can provide a high level of protection for any object, no matter what application the organization's personnel develops and runs against the integrated database.

Each object will be placed in a class determined by the level of protection required for that object. Each subject will be a member of a hierarchy. The hierarchical classifying of the subjects will allow subjects to create other subjects, while ensuring that the created subject will not have more privileges than its creator. Some of the subjects considered in the model are as follows:

- Database administrator
- Development teams
- System and application programmers
- Maintenance
- Operations
- Terminals
- Programs and utilities

Some of the objects considered in the model are the following:

- Programs and utilities
- Terminals
- Database files
- OS files
- Database segments
- Database fields
- Data dictionary entries

5.4.2   The Access Matrix — Case Study

A typical case of an application of the access matrix is shown in Figure 5-1.

EMP. NAME	EMP. ADDRESS	EMP. PHONE #	EMP. S.I.N.	EMP. EDUCA.	EMP. SAL HIST	EMP. MEDICAL	EMP. PENSION	
11	11	11	11	11	11	11	11	PERSONNEL
01	01	01	01	00	00	00	00	ACCOUNTING
00	00	00	00	00	00	00	00	MARKETING
00	00	00	00	00	00	00	00	PURCHASING
11	11	11	11	11	11	11	11	D.B.A.
10	10	10	10	10	10	10	10	MAINTENENCE
11	11	11	11	11	11	11	11	D.B.A.
10	10	10	10	10	10	10	10	MAINTENANCE
10	10	10	10	10	10	10	10	PROGRAMMERS
10	10	10	10	10	10	10	10	OPERATIONS
01	01	01	00	00	00	00	00	CLERICAL

Legend: 01–READ   00–NO ACCESS
         11–READ AND WRITE   10–WRITE ONLY

Figure 5-1   Typical Access Matrix

Each entry in the access matrix determines the access rights of the subjects to the objects. For example, the '01' in the first column and second row indicates that the ACCOUNTING department can READ the EMPLOYEE NAME; the '11' in the first column and row indicates that the PERSONNEL department can both READ and WRITE the EMPLOYEE NAME on the EMPLOYEE database; the '00' in the fifth column and second row indicates that the ACCOUNTING department can neither READ nor WRITE the EM-

PLOYEE EDUCATION information; and the '10' in the first column and sixth row indicates that the MAINTENANCE department can only write the EMPLOYEE NAME on the EMPLOYEE database.

The matrix can accommodate several other access attributes such as EXECUTE, DELETE, UPDATE, APPEND (add something to the end of a data item without altering its original contents), SORT, CREATE, and OWN. This can be accomplished by adding appropriate codes.

The elements of the access matrix usually contain bits that represent accesses that can be performed by the subject on the object. However, if desired, the elements may contain pointers to PROCEDURES, DIRECTORIES, or PROGRAMS. This feature is useful since programs or procedures contain greater processing capabilities than a simple WRITE command, for example.

The additional processing information from the procedures, directories, or programs will be made available at each attempted access by a given subject to a given object. The information will allow those access decisions that depend on information not easily represented in the access matrix to be made.

5.4.3 Rules Governing Accessing Decisions

The accessing decisions are governed by a set of rules listed below:

- A subject may transfer any access attribute it holds for an object to any other subject.
- A subject may grant to any subject access attributes for an object it owns.
- A subject may delete any access attribute from the column of an object it owns or the row of a subject it created.
- A subject may read the portion of the access matrix it owns or controls.
- A subject may create a nonsubject object. The creation of an object consists of adding a new column to the access matrix. The creator of the object is given "owner" access to the newly created object and may then grant access attributes to other subjects for their object.
- The owner of an object may destroy that object. This corresponds to deleting the column from the access matrix.
- A subject may create another subject. This consists of creating a row and column for the new subject in the access matrix, giving

the creator "owner" access to the new subject, and giving the new subject "control" access to itself.

- Only the "owner" may destroy a subject. This corresponds to deleting both the row and the column from the access matrix.
- Access may be based on the access history of other objects; subject A may write in object F only if he or she has not read from object G.
- Access may be based on the dynamic state of the system: subject B may read object H only at a time when the database in which the object resides is in a predetermined state.
- Access may be based on the prescribed usage of the object. A subject may sort an object in a protection level higher than that of the subject provided no date is returned to the subject.
- Access may be based on the current value of the object. A given subject may not read the salary field of any personnel record for which the salary value is greater than $20,000.
- Access may be based on the class of certain subjects: no access to a certain object can be made by a class of subjects between certain time period; e.g., between 12 a.m. and 8 a.m.
- Access may be based on the class of certain objects: certain terminals or portions of the database can't be accessed between 12 a.m. and 8 a.m.

The access matrix is really the heart of the security system. By including more information in it, the complex aspects of data security such as data-dependent checks can also be achieved.

5.4.4 Protection Levels of Access Matrix

In the access matrix described above authorization to the access object is based on the protection levels of the objects and the classification of the subjects. Access requests are denied unless the classification of the subject requesting access equals or exceeds the protection level of the object requested.

Access can be controlled beyond the file level of the database if desired. By using directories that allow access to other directories and eventually to actual files, hierarchies of successively more restrictive access can be set up. This approach will provide adequate protection at the field level of the database.

The protection level of each object will be determined by the team that does the risk analysis. Each protection level will then be assigned to a directory. The movement of an object from one directory to another will indicate that the protection level of that object has been either increased or decreased.

The protection levels of the model will be increased as the need for more security is uncovered. Some levels that may be considered are as follows:

- No sharing at all (complete isolation)
- Sharing copies of programs, files, or the database
- Sharing originals of programs, files, or the database
- Sharing entire programming systems
- Permitting the cooperation of mutually suspicious systems
- Providing subsystems with the ability to perform a task but guaranteeing that no secret records of or from that task are kept by subsystems

5.4.5   The Access Matrix Monitor

The monitor of the access matrix is that part of the software that ensures that there is no violation of the protection levels of the objects. It should be designed in such a way that any attempted violation of the protection levels or the database will trigger an audit or logging capability. In order to accomplish this one must ensure that there can be no unauthorized alteration of the monitor.

The monitor can either be some software mechanism or administrative control which validates and then permits or denies each and every request for access to protectable objects.

A security program is effective to the extent it reaches and affects all elements of the organization. One of the most effective mechanisms for assuring widespread distribution and uniform enforcement of security policy is through an existing or newly created standards program. A good standard can be defined as a precept that is enforced because the benefits outweigh the costs.

When initially developing a computer security program, it is essential that meaningful policy and standards be set forth and disseminated to all personnel, so that each individual is fully aware of mandatory security requirements.

As a minimum, these standards should address the following areas:

- Background of security policy
- Purpose

- Responsibilities for security
- Personnel security
- Physical access controls
- Media and facility protection
- Communication and network security
- Hardware and software
- Password control
- Controlling release of sensitive data
- Integrity controls and error detection
- Security violation

Before dissemination to the organization as a working document, standards must be fully coordinated among the various organization departments.

Procedures are more definitive: They provide step-by-step directions for performing a course of action. They should be specific and oriented to a given task in a given department.

Security procedures should be detailed enough to be usable as a working document. For example, procedures regarding password changes should read, "passwords will be changed by system administrator at least once per month" and not, "passwords will be changed regularly."

In any organization, probably the most difficult aspect of security procedure is enforcement. It is one thing to declare that the programmers will not leave an online terminal unattended, but quite another problem to enforce the rule. In this regard, security procedures should be subjected to the three rules of effectiveness:

- Economic feasibility — Are the procedures too costly?
- Operational feasibility — A 10-digit password might be secure, but is it a reasonable solution?
- Technical feasibility — Can the procedure be implemented with the existing technical knowledge and equipment?

5.4.6 Administrative Controls in Access Matrix Environment

The organization about to use the access matrix should develop policies and standards that will form the basis of the administrative controls that can assist the access matrix in its efforts to deny or grant access to protectable objects. If adequate controls exist, attempts at unauthorized access may be thwarted before they enter the computer system.

Interviews should be conducted with data security personnel to determine what procedures are already in place to control subjects' requests to resources.

All aspects of the requesting process should be examined and the adequacy of the existing controls evaluated. It is hoped that the study will lead to new controls that will reflect the current environment and need for adequate data security.

5.4.7   The Software Version of the Access Matrix Monitor

The monitor, the part of the access matrix model that enforces the security policy, should be designed according to the following three principles:

- Complete mediation — the monitor must mediate every access of a subject to an object
- Isolation — the monitor and its database must be protected from unauthorized alteration
- Verifiability — the monitor must be small, simple, and understandable so that it can be completely tested and verified to perform its functions correctly

5.4.8   Design of the Monitor

Some considerations in the design of the monitor are as follows:

- Interfacing between the monitor and other parts of the system such as user programs
- How control is to be passed across the interface — in terms of invoking or calling the monitor
- Means of identifying processes that interact with the monitor
- Means of queuing and assigning priorities to request for services of the monitor
- Interfacing of the monitor with other auditing programs
- Protection of monitor against modification
- Interfacing of the monitor with subject and object directories

5.4.9   Functions of Monitor

The main functions of the monitor can be listed as follows:

- Responsible for creating and deleting subjects and objects
- Creates a process containing the subject id, the object's protection level, and associated access attributes
- Terminates the subject's process and cleans up on his behalf
- Releases all reserved objects, closes any objects that are opened, removes the subject from the request queue, and purges the portion of memory that acted as the work area
- Maintains data consistency and seeks to avoid or resolve data interference
- Reserves and holds objects

5.4.10   Design of Subject and Object Directories

The directories to be established for the access matrix model will include the following:

- Information on subjects
- Information on objects
- Protection levels
- Pointers to other directories

5.5   Objects and Subjects of the Access Matrix

The subjects of the matrix should be members of a hierarchy and have functions in relation to that hierarchy. For example, the DBA could be the universal subject and have the following functions:

- Establish new subjects
- Impose logical limits on the resources
- Remove subject's ability to access the database
- Determine maximum protection level of each subject
- Define resource limitation of each subject
- Monitor and display all subjects and protection levels of objects
- Reclassify a subject
- Reclassify an object

The objects of the matrix must have a unique identifier, access attributes, description, and value set. The access attributes can be any of the following: READ, WRITE, UPDATE, etc. The description must indicate the format, size, and creation and last update information.

5.5.1 Processing Details of Access Matrix Model

Figure 5-2 outlines the processing components of the access matrix system.
A request to access an object will undergo the following steps:

• User program or transaction makes a request to access a protectable object to the monitor.
• Monitor checks user program (subject) identifier, retrieves access matrix row containing the object to which access is requested.
• Access matrix points to relevant directory.
• Monitor gets relevant information about subject and object from directory.
• Monitor verifies that the subject is authorized to access the requested object.

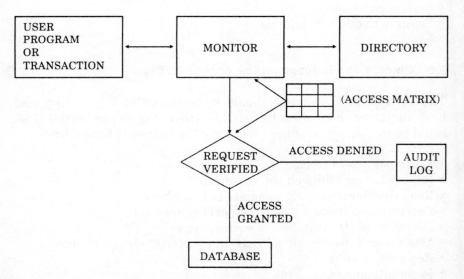

Figure 5-2 Schematic of Components of the Access Matrix Control System

• Decision about request is made by the monitor. If request is denied, the monitor triggers an online terminal, which creates an audit trail or log. If request is granted, the monitor accesses the database and returns the requested data item to the user program.

5.5.2 Processing Alternatives of Access Matrix Model

The design of the monitor is very critical in cutting down on overhead during processing. The monitor should be flexible enough to incorporate some of the following processing alternatives:

• Monitor should be able to determine whether the class of subjects making a request is authorized to access the requested object. This would prevent having to get the information from the access matrix or the directory.
• Monitor should be able to make determinations from either the access matrix or the directory and not necessarily have to access both.
• Monitor should be able to go directly to the database, bypassing access matrix and directories, after request is verified.
• Monitor should be able to update directories and put special emphasis on history (time)-sensitive information.

5.6 Risk Assessment as an Aid to Selecting a Protection Mechanism

Many organizations hesitate to initiate a security program because of their ignorance of the sensitivity of the data in their environment and the cost/benefit in instituting security features. This ignorance exists mainly due to reluctance of the organization to conduct risk analysis. Many organizations institute security features only after a break in security occurs.

The purpose of performing a risk assessment is to obtain a quantitative statement of the potential problems to which the data processing facility is exposed, so the appropriate cost-effective security safeguards can be selected. It is assumed that, once armed with such information, no security measure will be selected that costs more than tolerating the problem. The risk assessment should establish that threshold.

The risk analysis provides a rational approach toward choosing security safeguards. A security program should logically provide protection in the most economical manner. The following questions, therefore, should be answered in the course of a risk assessment:

- What are the specific results desired; that is, exactly how much security is required?
- What is the proper balance between security program cost and potential benefits?
- When trade-offs can be made between protection and recovery, how much effort should be expended on each?

An important part of the security program involves determining what functions are performed or supported by the database environment that is vital to the organization's survival. The advisability of providing security beyond this minimum can be determined largely through the cost/benefit analysis.

Freedom of information legislation may require organizations to allow their customers access to their records. How such requests would affect the current structure of the organization's database can be determined only by a risk assessment.

Any risk assessment conducted at an early developmental stage of database design will be less costly and will allow more adequate security features to be built into developing systems at a lower cost than at a later stage, when systems are completed and may have to go through tremendous redesign phases and cost to implement similar and necessary security features.

The risk assessment conducted by corporations at an early stage of development need not be expensive. A useful set of baseline data can be obtained by conducting simple interviews and surveys in all departments and data processing groups.

5.7 Resource Access Control Facility (RACF) as a Protection Mechanism

RACF is a program product from IBM that is designed to identify system users and control their access to protected resources.

RACF's authorization structure can be contrasted with a data set password mechanism. With typical password protection, a password is assigned to a specific data set. The system ensures that the date set can be accessed only when that password is supplied.

Protected data sets can be accessed by anyone who knows the password. Obviously, there are control problems associated with restricting knowledge of the passwords.

There are also problems in withdrawing access to data sets. If three people know the password for a particular data set and an administrator wants to take away one person's access rights, the password must be changed and the new password communicated to the users.

5.7.1 RACF Concepts

The RACF authorization structure is based on principles different from password protection. RACF eliminates the need for data set passwords.

With RACF, an administrator or auditor can tell which users are authorized to access which data sets. A user's right to access data set can be withdrawn simply by changing the structure.

The RACF authorization structure contains three kinds of elements: users, groups of users, and protected resources. It stores descriptions of users, groups, and resources in profiles contained in a special data set called the RACF data set. The types of resources that RACF protects are direct-access storage device (DASD) data sets, tape volumes, DASD volumes, terminals, and applications.

Users, groups, and resources can be interrelated. A user can be a member of one or more groups. This membership allows the user to administer the group or simply to function within the group when accessing data. Both users and groups can be authorized to access protected resources. The type of access allowed corresponds to the different types of operations that can be performed in data handling.

RACF interfaces with the operating system in three main areas:

• Identification and verification of users
• Authorization checking for access to protect resources
• Monitoring to provide both immediate notification of security problems and a log for post de facto analysis

Once RACF has verified the user's identity, it builds a description of the user. This description is kept in memory for the duration of the job or online session. Comparing this description with what the user can do is the basis for authority checking.

Authority checking is the basis for deciding whether a processing function or an access to RACF performs authority checking without any user or operator intervention. If the access is authorized, it is allowed; if unauthorized, it is denied.

RACF follows very specific rules for authority verification. First, it checks to see if the user is authorized to the resource by inspecting the resource profile in the RACF data set. If this is not the case, then RACF uses its description of the protected resource. RACF determines if the user is on the access list. If he is, then RACF can decide whether the user should be authorized to perform the function he has requested.

If the user is not on the access list, RACF then checks to see if the user's group is on the access list.

Monitoring or logging is used to record and subsequently report the occurrence of unauthorized access attempts. It also serves to provide evidence that the general security guidelines that have been implemented are being enforced. RACF uses two general types of monitoring:

- Logging if access to data or to the system
- Logging if changes to the RACF profiles that define the authorization structures

If an access attempt is unauthorized, it will not be permitted or the profile change will not take place. Depending upon options set by administrators or by the resource owner, a log record will be written, and a message will be set to a designated security console.

The log record contains the following:

- Normal time stamp
- Identification of the user and group causing the action being logged
- Levels of authority required and granted
- Identification of the resource in question
- Operands specified and the values specified for these operands when the RACF profiles are changed

5.8 Summary

This chapter discussed some of the advanced features of database security, privacy, and integrity. It covered the need for management's involvement in and support of any effort in data security, a risk assessment to determine the sensitivity of the organization's data, and audit trails to determine who did what and when in terms of breaching the security.

We discussed two protection mechanisms: the access matrix developed by the author and the Resource Access Control Facility (RACF) developed by IBM. The chapter concluded by giving a detailed account of these protection mechanisms for the benefit of researchers interested in installing any of them in their organization.

6

Management, Planning, and Control of the Database

Introduction

In an earlier chapter, I established the premise that data is a resource in much the same way as employees, products, natural resources, finances, and other material products or resources.

In the same chapter, I defined information resource management (IRM) as a discipline that deals with planning for, allocating, maintaining and conserving, prudently exploiting, effectively employing, and integrating the data resource.

This chapter deals with three aspects of IRM. It deals with the effective management of the data resource. It emphasizes the fact that in order to effectively manage data, it is necessary to obtain as much data about the data resource as possible. It deals with planning for the data resource. In planning for this resource, I emphasize the strategic, tactical, and operational aspects of IRM planning. In the area of control of the data resource, it deals with establishing lines of authority and responsibility for the data. It emphasizes the importance of having common procedures for collecting, updating, and maintaining the data. Finally, it establishes that in order to control the data resource, the organization must evaluate, mediate, and reconcile the conflicting needs and prerogatives of its functional departments.

6.1   Management of the Data Resource

In order to manage data effectively as a resource, it is necessary to obtain as much data about the data resource as possible. There must be stringent procedures for collecting, maintaining, and using the resource. The next several sections will discuss various tools that can be used in the effective management of the data resource.

6.1.1   The Data Dictionary

The data dictionary may be defined as an organized reference to the data content of an organization's programs, systems, databases, collections of all files, or manual records.

The data dictionary may be maintained manually or by a computer. Sometimes, the term "data dictionary" may refer to a software product that is utilized to maintain a dictionary database. The data dictionary will contain names, descriptions, and definitions of the organization's data resource.

6.1.2   The Data Dictionary as a Management Tool

The data dictionary is perhaps the most important tool that information resource managers have at their disposal. The data dictionary allows management to document and support application development and assist in designing and controlling the database environment. It allows managers to set standards and monitor adherence to those standards.

In the database environment, the data dictionary can be used to document the single-user view of the organization's data or several integrated views. It can document the related data models of those views, the logical databases that results from those views, and the physical representation of those logical models.

The organization can store complete representations of its data architecture in the data dictionary. This data architecture can be used to indicate how adequately the data resource supports the business functions of the organization and also show what data the company will need to support its long-range plans for expansion.

The dictionary allows information managers to respond quickly to upper-level management's needs for data in a decision support environment. It supports the organization's need for consistent data definitions and usage.

The data dictionary can be used to indicate management's desire to control access to the organization's data resource. Managers can now state who can access the data and the level of access assigned to the individual. They can use the data dictionary, in consort with the operating system, to deny access to unauthorized individuals.

The data dictionary can provide managers and other users with concise definitions of entities and data items that are important to the organization. It can indicate where data is used, what uses it, how it is used, and other dependencies on that data.

Management can indicate, via the dictionary, who is responsible for changing the characteristics of the data resource and the procedures for effecting the change. On the other hand, managers can use the dictionary to control changes to the data resource and readily assess the effect on systems, programs, and user operations when such changes are made.

6.1.3   The Database as a Management Tool

Today's highly competitive business climate, characterized by more educated consumers and shorter product cycles, forces companies to be information driven. Corporate decision makers derive information by analyzing raw data, gathered internally or externally, in a particular business context. Therefore, to be successful, a company must ensure that this raw data is captured and readily available for analysis in various forms. If such data is easily accessible, various levels of support must be built before meaningful information can be obtained.

Various tools have evolved over the past two decades to facilitate data resource management. When first introduced, database management systems (DBMS) were thought to offer a panacea to the growing lack of control over the company data resources.

The database can be defined as a collection of interrelated data items processable by one or more application systems. The database permits common data to be integrated and shared between corporate functional units and provides flexibility of data organization. It facilitates the addition of data to an existing database without modification of existing application programs. This data independence is achieved by removing the direct association between the application program and physical storage of data.

The advantages of the database are:

* Consistency through use of the same data by all corporate parts.
* Application program independence from data sequence and structure.
* Reduction and control of redundant data.
* Reduction in application development costs, storage costs, and processing costs.

Database technology has permitted information resource managers to organize data around subjects that interest the company. It has allowed for data sharing among divergent parts of the organization. It has introduced new methods of managing data and new and sophisticated logical and physical design methodologies. By having a central pool of data, the organization can now secure the resource more efficiently and in more cost-effective ways. Access to the data can be more readily controlled while making it available to a wider audience of diverse users.

The technology has allowed management, through decision support systems (DSS), to more readily adjust to the changed environment of their respective businesses and reduce the impact of these changes on the organization's economy.

6.1.4 Managing the Corporate Database

Effective management of the corporate database requires that the following activities be addressed consistently and logically:

* Planning — The corporate database must be planned according to the specific needs of the company.
* Organization — A data-driven company requires new organizational entities.
* Acquisition — Once the corporate database has been planned, the needed data must be acquired.
* Maintenance and Control — The data in the corporate database must be securely, accurately, and completely maintained. In addition, proper control must be exercised over access to the database. Data ownership, use, and custodianship issues must also be addressed.
* Usage — The corporate database must be available to all authorized users in the company.

A. Planning

Planning entails the preparation of all corporate data models. This is best achieved through interviews with the department heads of each functional area in the company. These managers should be asked to determine what data influences their functional areas and what information is required to successfully operate and manage their departments. After all the interviews are completed, the collection of data items must be analyzed and distilled into a model that can be understood, presented, and accepted by corporate management. This analysis should include a determination of the source of the data as well as its characteristics and interrelationships with other data items. This corporate data model must then be compared with currently held and maintained data. The difference between what is currently available and what is ultimately required determines what data must be collected.

B. Organization

There are two distinct aspects of organizing the corporate database. The first is the business aspect — identifying which data is relevant to the company, its source and method of capture, and the interrelationships among the data items. The second is the technical aspect — storing data on computer-readable media in a form readily accessible by the corporate decision makers. The business tasks of organizing the corporate database required the creation of the relatively new chief information officer (CIO) and the more traditional data administration function.

The CIO is the executive in charge of the information systems department and is responsible for formulating an information strategy that includes all systems development, computer operations, and communications planning and operation.

The data administration function links computer systems and the business functions they are designed to serve. The group responsible for data administration builds and maintains the corporate data model. A properly constructed data model places the system to be developed into a proper business perspective. This model is instrumental in the preparation of the information systems department's strategic plan.

C. Acquisition

In a data-driven organization, information strategy is derived from the corporate data model. Systems planned for development should provide information or a level of service that was previously unavailable. In a typical systems development project, a major part of the effort is spent in acquiring and storing the data that is used to produce the required information.

Although data analysis and design is defined as a separate activity in the definition of data resource management, application programs to collect and validate data items and add them to the appropriate database must still be written. The interactions among systems development, data administration, and database administration must be in place to ensure that the corporate database effectively acquires data.

D. Maintenance and Control

Maintenance tasks include making changes to the corporate data model, reflecting these changes in the data dictionary, and properly communicating them to all users who must know the model's current status. Given the degree of data independence that can be achieved in today's DBMSs, changes to the database should not necessitate changes to application programs. However, the addition of new data items and changes or deletions to existing data items must be controlled as vigorously as changes to application systems. That is, the change control principles applied to application programs must be applied to changes in data definitions used by these programs.

Data security issues are critical in data-driven organizations. The data is used and relied upon by all corporate users, including high-level decision makers. Procedures must be established that define what level of access an individual should be granted. Unauthorized access must be detected and reported. The cause of the infraction also must be determined, and action taken to prevent its reoccurrence.

The distinction must be made between data owners — those with update authority — and data users — those with read-only access or limited update authority.

The computer operations group is the custodian of all data. This group must ensure that proper monitoring is performed, and that backup and recovery procedures are in place and functioning. The data administrator should also have sufficient authority to arbitrate any ownership disputes between rival users.

Maintenance and control activities should also monitor systems performance and the time required to access needed data items. The database administration group should monitor system performance and take whatever corrective action is needed to provide an adequate level of response to users or systems requiring access to particular data items.

E. Usage

Procedures that clearly define how to use the database must be established. First, potential users must know what data exists. Then, tools must be provided to enable users to easily access selected data items. For example, query languages that provide flexible database access and allow what-if questions to be presented and answered are implemented in many companies. Another area of great potential is the ability to interface selected data items with business software tools. These interfaces provide users with more meaningful presentations of the extracted information.

The delivery vehicle used to bring the data to the users must also be considered. Many companies have established information centers to provide a user-friendly environment for data access. This access may be provided through interactive query languages that enable users to view results online or through batch report generators that enable users to obtain preformatted printed reports.

Downloading segments of the database to a microcomputer is another method of information delivery that is becoming more common. The microcomputer environment typically provides the user with interactive access to the data as well as easy-to-use and powerful software. With the continuing emergence of local area networks (LANs), more and more data will be downloaded to microcomputers for use by the end-user community.

6.1.5 The Data Model as a Management Tool

A data model is defined as a logical representation of a collection of data elements and the associations among those data elements. A data model can be used to represent data usage throughout an organization or can represent a single database structure. A data model is to data what a logical data flow diagram is to a process.

The data model can be used by management to:

• Develop new systems
• Maintain existing systems
• Develop data structures for the entire organization

• Prioritize the data needs of the organization
• Assist in planning for expansion into new markets or business areas
• Delegate authority for data usage
• Classify data by data areas or business functions
• Determine security needs of the data and implement protection mechanisms

A. Develop New Systems

Data models are fast becoming a very important tool in the development of new systems in an organization. The advent of new structured design methodologies, especially data-driven methodologies, saw the birth of data models as tools for systems development. The traditional approach to developing computer systems focuses on the processes to be performed, particularly with operational-type systems. However, process-oriented system designs generally do not fulfill subsequent tactical or strategic information needs. In many cases, information requests go unanswered because either the source data does not exist or custom building software that supports ad hoc inquiries is too costly and time-consuming. This accurate information is a major disadvantage of many conventional systems.

The data resource management approach overcomes this limitation by focusing on data and information requirements during systems planning and building. The data model now becomes the vehicle by which application systems are built while addressing these limitations.

B. Maintain Existing Systems

It has been determined that 80 percent of an organization's programming resources is expended during maintenance on existing systems. This expenditure is consumed by programmers trying to determine where changes should be made to existing systems and what data is best suited to test the modified programs. The expenditure may even occur before the changes are made. Programmers may spend, depending upon their experience, a considerable amount of time determining how the application meets the requirements of the business function. This expenditure in time and financial resources can be minimized if there are data models of all existing systems in place.

The programmers can determine from the data models the section or user view that must be modified. Then, with the data model section or user view as a guide, the parts of the application programs that must be changed will be more readily identified and programming maintenance expenditure would be less costly.

C. Develop Data Structures for the Organization

The organization, by undertaking a business system plan (BSP), can identify business processes and data classes required to design databases for its informational needs. Various charts showing the relationship between business processes and classes of data can be prepared. This relationship is the backbone of the data architecture for the organization. The data architecture, in turn, is obtained through a single data model or set of data models.

D. Prioritize the Data Needs of the Organization

It is impossible in most organizations to implement systems to satisfy all data needs at once. Priorities must be set and phased implementation of these systems undertaken. The data model can show what data is available, where it is available, and where it is needed. Data managers can use this information to determine the cost and complexity of implementation of systems, and hence prioritize the implementation of these systems.

E. Assist in planning for Expansion of Business

Whenever an organization expands its business into new markets or business areas, data is needed to aid or even implement the expansion. Data models are very useful tools that management can use to determine what data is needed and where it can be obtained for the expansion program.

F. Delegate Authority for Data Usage

Data models can indicate to an organization what business function uses what data. They can also be used to indicate the common uses and functions of corporate data. Corporate management can use this information to delegate authority for data usage throughout the organization. Managers can also use this information to control access, on a need-to-know basis, to the corporate data.

G. Classify Data by Data Areas

Data is very often classified by the business function it serves. For example, data that serves an accounting function is very often classified as accounting data. Data models, by showing the relationship between business functions and business entities (data), can assist in the proper classification of corporate data.

H. Determine Security Needs of Data

Data models allow an organization to determine what data is available, who uses it, and where it is being used. They allow the organization to determine the common usage of data and the parameters that are needed to allow data usage across organizational boundaries. Armed with this knowledge, an organization can now plan for its data security needs. It can determine what protection mechanisms are needed to control access to the data and the level of authorization to be given to users of corporate data.

6.1.6   Data Flow Diagrams as a Management Tool

Data flow diagrams assist the systems analysts in determining where data is being held from one transaction to the next, or stored permanently because it describes some aspect of the world outside the system. They indicate how the data flows from process to process. They assist the analysts in determining what immediate accesses to each data store will be needed by the user.

Data flow diagrams are powerful tools that can be used by organizations to develop process-flow architectures for their environment. Management can use this tool to determine where data is created, where it is being used, and who uses the informational contents.

Management can use the data flow diagrams to build complete databases to store the required data for users' needs. They can use the processes to transform flows of data. The processes can be decomposed into functions and activities from which programs can be coded to manipulate the data stores.

Data flow diagrams are currently being used on a worldwide basis as the major deliverable from process-driven structured systems analysis and development. Several organizations are using data flow diagrams as a deliverable of a basic business systems plan (BSP). Data flow diagrams are also being used by several organizations to demonstrate and illustrate their corporate data needs.

Management can use the ability to break down processes into several levels to determine the operational processing requirements of each data store in the process architecture. For example, one organization is currently using data flow diagrams to determine whether operational processing, such as sorting, dumping to other storage media, deleting of files, and creating of backup files, is consuming too much of the corporation's operational budgets and time. This same organization is using data flow diagrams to illustrate where various reports are distributed to other users, whether current users should have access to the reports, and where reports are produced but never distributed.

Management can use existing data flow diagrams to audit the corporate data dictionary for completeness and currency. For example, a complete data dictionary should have data about all the processes and data stores that exist in the organization. By checking the data dictionary content against existing data flow diagrams, the completeness of the data dictionary can be determined. The assumption here is that the data flow diagrams are in themselves complete and represent the entire information and process architecture of the corporation.

Data flow diagrams can be used to create functional specifications for systems development. The data flow diagram shows the sources and distinctions of data and hence indicates the boundaries of the system. It identifies and names the logical functions, the data elements that connect the function to another, and the data stores each function accesses. Each data flow is analyzed, its structures and the definitions of its component data elements stored in the data dictionary. Each logical function may be broken down into a more detailed data flow diagram. The contents of each data store are analyzed and stored in the data dictionary.

These documents make up a comprehensive account of a system that can be used by management to build systems or prioritize the building of systems. The documents and the data flow diagrams may also prove very useful in the maintenance of existing systems.

Finally, data flow diagrams can be used by systems designers to prepare functional specifications that are:

- Well understood and fully agreed to by users
- Used to set out the logical requirements of the system without dictating a physical implementation
- Useful in expressing preferences and trade-offs

Several organizations are attesting to the fact that data flow diagrams can prevent very costly errors in systems development. Figure 6-1 is an example of a data flow diagram.

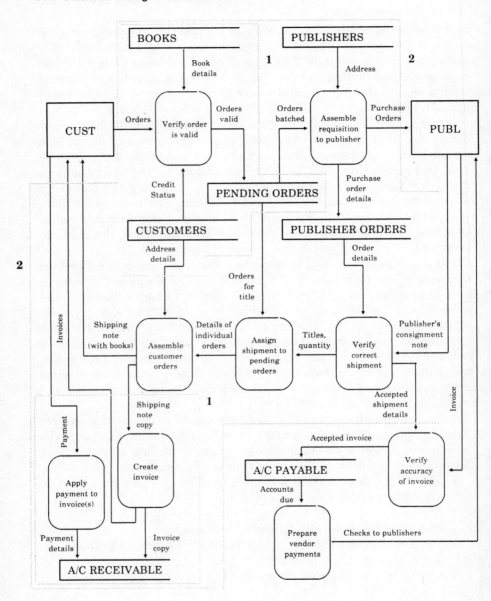

Figure 6-1   Illustration of a Data Flow Diagram

6.1.7   Managing Information Through CASE Tools

More and more organizations are looking to CASE tools to improve the effectiveness of analysts and designers, increase the role of end users in systems design, reduce programming and maintenance time, and manage data more effectively.

Computer-aided software engineering (CASE) is the automation of software development. CASE is a combination of software tools and systems development methodologies. CASE is different from earlier software technologies because it focuses on the entire software productivity problem, not just on implementation solutions. CASE attacks software productivity problems at both ends of the life cycle by automating many analysis and design tasks, as well as program implementation and maintenance tasks.

CASE offers full support for the systems development life cycle. At the analysis phase, CASE allows the designer to collect user requirements through conventional interview methods or by the use of Structure English. The collected user requirements are entered into a CASE repository or data dictionary and become the input to the design phase. The deliverables from the design phase can be data models, such as entity-relationship diagrams or data flow diagrams. The tools have the ability to explode the data flow diagrams down to several levels and balance the data stores at each level. The deliverables are checked against the data dictionary entries for accuracy, consistency, and completeness.

Most of the CASE tools have a prototyping capability and can create screens of the user requirements and models of the systems so that users can review the design at a very early stage of systems development. During prototyping, simulated reports can be produced that reflect the actual reports required by the users.

CASE tools use the entries in the data dictionary and the processes from the design phase not only to develop programming specifications for application programmers but even to generate the actual program code compatible with standards for several programming languages.

At the moment, the major weakness of CASE tools is their inability to maintain program code and changes to existing systems over the life of the system. Several manufacturers of CASE tools are now developing solutions to this problem, and the answers may not be too far off.

CASE tools have become very important tools for managers to use in their efforts to manage data more effectively and prudently exploit the data resource. They now represent the most rapidly growing sector of the software industry. CASE tools — what they are and how they should be selected — is the topic of Chapter 11.

6.1.8   Managing Information Through Reverse Engineering

Reverse engineering is defined as the act of taking unstructured programs or systems not designed using one of the current structured design methodologies, and either structuring the programs or producing deliverables more appropriate to the structured systems development life cycle (SDLC).

Reverse engineering accomplishes the following:

- Produces programs that are structured and now less costly, both in time and money, to maintain
- Enhances the quality of programs, program documentation, and informational content
- Increases the useful life of program code and identifies sections of programs that can be reused as subroutines
- Removes or identifies unreachable or unexecutable codes in programs
- Indicates problem areas in unstructured programs which could be responsible for seemingly inexplicable processing behavior

Although most of the effort of reverse engineering is now centered on producing structured program code from unstructured code, a considerable amount of effort is now being expended in producing deliverables more appropriate with a structured SDLC. For example, there are efforts being undertaken to produce entity-relationship (E-R) diagrams from the data division of Cobol programs. These E-R diagrams are then used along with the major processes defined by the Cobol programs to populate data dictionaries, produce logical and physical design schemas, provide better documentation for programming specifications and maintenance, and build relevant databases. Managers can now use the data dictionary content, the documentation, and the databases to more effectively manage the data resource.

6.1.9   Project Management Tools and Management of Data

There are now several automated project management tools on the market that seek to aid in the development of systems and indirectly in the management of data.

Project management tools are used in the following areas:

- Project planning
- Project duration
- Costing
- Manpower scheduling
- Manpower allocation
- Project reporting

6.2   Planning for the Data Resource

Planning for the data resource is done at three levels: strategic, tactical, and operational.

A. Strategic Planning — Defines the data environment's mission and objective in achieving the goals of the organization. The strategic plan is driven by the current and future information needs of the business. Strategic planning helps businesses share the data resource.

The strategic data plan defines the organization's data requirements and states the benefits of data resource management and how it differs from database technology management. The strategic plan serves as the baseline for data resource management and directs all subsequent data-related activities.

The strategic plan defines the target toward which all subsequent data-related activity is directed.

B. Tactical Planning — Identifies a resource and directs the way in which it will be managed to achieve goals set forth in the strategic plan. Because each resource is to be managed in its own life cycle, each should ideally be governed by its own plan. The tactical planning window is 12–18 months, with a review cycle of 9–12 months.

C. Operational Planning — Describes the details of the tactical plan and identifies the tasks to be carried out in a scheduled time frame, the expected deliverables, and the assigned responsibilities. The window operational planning is 3–9 months, depending on the size of the project.

6.2.1   Contents of the Strategic Plan

The strategic plan should address the broadest context under which data sharing will exist and should contain the following sections:

- The purpose of the data resource
- Goals for supporting the information strategies of the organization
- Strategies that pursue the goals
- Factors critical to achieving the goals successfully
- Constraints imposed on the data environment
- The concepts of data resource management
- The resources needed to manage data

A. Mission Statement — Reflects an overall direction for data resource management from a single, high-level perspective. It defines the scope of the data environment. For example, a mission statement may read as follows: To provide data about shared corporate entities to all regional offices in a timely and controlled manner.

B. Goals — Identify expected results to be gained in that domain. For example, a goal of data resource management may be to build a strategic data architecture that will ensure the integrity of data as it is integrated across application systems.

C. Strategies — Are general statements of direction for achieving data resource management goals. Strategies are generally applied across goals to identify how the goals will be achieved. For example, a strategy for data resource management may be to train systems staff and end users in data-oriented systems design and database development or to provide effective data security with minimal interruption to end-user service.

D. Critical Success Factors — Are broad statements of achievements in data resource management. For example, a critical success factor may be the management of data through a data dictionary. Success is achieved with the implementation and effective use of the data dictionary.

E. Constraints — Data resource management may be constrained by the evolution of the business, the state of the technology in the environment, and the availability of staff. Current business operations and the role of information in the organization's planning may force constraints on the scope of data resource management.

Planning for the data resource must include acquisition of data through application systems, employment and exploitation of data through end-user reports, maintenance of data through the technology tools, and disposition of the data depending on the life cycle of the business subject matter. The deletion of the data element is determined by its relationship to other elements.

Planning for the data resource must identify the tools to manage the data resource, including database management systems, data dictionaries, data modeling tools, CASE tools, and database auditing, journaling, and recovery tools.

6.3   Controlling the Data Resource

The third component of information resource management is the control of the data resource. Although the other two components, management and planning, were discussed first, this is no indication of their relative importance in the triumvirate.

Management control of the data resource includes the following:

- Common procedures for access control to the data
- Establishing lines of authority and responsibility for the data
- Common procedures for access control to the data
- Establishing lines of authority and responsibility for the data
- Common procedures for collecting, updating, and maintaining the data
- Common formats and procedures for data definition
- Identifying entities that are important to the enterprise
- Evaluating, mediating, and reconciling the conflicting needs and prerogatives of functional departments
- Ensuring the auditability of the data and all transactions against the data
- Controlling the data in order to measure and evaluate the corporation and predict its reaction to change in its environment and in its own internal organization

The above list, although quite extensive, is by no means all-inclusive. I will leave the readers to expand on this list and also to research the various activities that must be performed to materialize each item in the list.

7

Concepts of Data Dictionaries

Introduction

Over the past several years, the data dictionary has been used as a tool by data administrators to document and maintain the names and definitions of the data items in the database. However, with the increasing recognition of data as a corporate resource and the need to manage the resources more efficiently, data administrators are putting the data dictionary to several different uses.

7.1 Data Dictionary as a Glossary of Definitions

One use of the data dictionary is as a glossary of terms, whether about the entire organization or for entire systems. The glossary allows users to communicate with one another using common terms and definitions.

The data dictionary can also be used as a glossary of data items. In this case, a few lines or few paragraphs are dedicated to defining the data items used in the database environment.

7.2   Data Dictionary as a System Development and Maintenance Tool

The data dictionary can be very effective when used as a tool to support structured analysis and design. It can be used to document data items, data flow, and process definitions. As such, it is an efficient way of portraying system design details to the user.

The data dictionary can also be used to generate file, segment, and record definitions for a variety of programming languages. By doing so, we can centralize the control of program data definitions. This will ensure consistency of data use and inhibit data redundancy.

Because we can centralize the control of data use, the data dictionary can be a very effective tool in change-control management. The data dictionary is the origin of all data definitions, and so any new data requirements must have the knowledge and approval of data administration.

Because the dictionary enforces consistency of data naming and format variation, it significantly reduces the cost of program maintenance.

7.3   Data Dictionary as a Superior Documentation Medium

Documentation stored in a data dictionary is available to anyone who has access to a computer terminal (and is properly authorized for access). The automated search and cross-referencing tools of a data dictionary can span multiple programs, systems, databases, report definitions, form definitions, or any other entity type.

The data dictionary can be used to generate the source program data definitions; the data portion of the program is actually derived from the documentation.

7.4   Case Histories of Data Dictionary Use

Company A is a large leading energy company in New York City. This company's database administration department has been evolving since 1976. The stated objectives of DBA are:

• Data is an important shared resource that should be managed and controlled just like other major corporate resources.

- Knowledge on how data and information are generated and used should become widely disseminated.
- Control should be exercised over the quality of the data resource to increase its effective utilization.

The DBA function exerts control over the data resources through management control of application development, test, and production environments. The company's DBA function sees its proper role as a full-time participant in the planning, design, and operation of database systems, with a view to ensuring that adequate features and appropriate data safeguards are provided.

In all these efforts, the manager of database administration sees the data dictionary as the primary tool for his function. The data dictionary is being used to organize the collection, storage, and retrieval of information about data.

7.4.1   Data Dictionary Use at Company A

The facilities of Company A's data dictionary are useful to all system development projects, nondatabase as well as database. The main thrust is to capture information describing data items and their attributes, highlighting their interrelationships. Functional analysis is also supported by the dictionary, based on its ability to define business activities in a machine-readable form.

The data dictionary is a tool that enables the DBA function to:

- Clarify and design data structures
- Avoid unwanted data redundancies
- Generate accurate and dependable data definitions
- Assess the impact of proposed computer system changes
- Enforce standards related to data

Because of the interest in management uses of data, the DBA function looks to see what management type data can be provided by each new application system. The DBA introduces appropriate integrated database designs that minimize the need for special processing to make that data suitable for current and future management uses.

7.4.2   Example of Management Uses of the Data Dictionary

An example of management use of the data dictionary is the Human Resources Information System (HURIS). Now under development, this system will establish a single source of people data within the company, servicing such application functions as payroll, employee relations, benefit plans, and so on. In addition to their ongoing review function and assistance in database design and installation, the DBA function developed a control monitor that supports an unusually flexible security apparatus, as well as an online report request and distribution system for end users.

7.4.3   Company A Approach to Using the Data Dictionary

The first step in Company A's approach to using the data dictionary was to acquire the basic dictionary capabilities and train the DBA staff members in their use. Then, corporate policies were established that required dictionary use for all database projects. The DBA is now in the process of developing additional tools, procedures, and educational materials to enhance the usefulness of the data dictionary.

Ultimately, the DBA function must impose a discipline on data content and not just its form. His staff must coordinate the definition of all data that crosses departmental boundaries; for data that is used only by one department, there is less need to impose standards. The DBA function needs to clean up the existing data definitions and then monitor all additions, deletions, and changes to these definitions.

In the long run, the monitoring and editing of data definitions are essential if data resources are to become truly shareable. The editing of key data definitions found in all application systems is a very large undertaking, so this step should be approached somewhat cautiously.

7.4.4   Company A's Use of the Data Dictionary for Business Planning

An area of current interest is the mechanism by which the DBA function can support business planning. Beginning with the business objectives, the business processes needed to support these objectives are identified and recorded in the dictionary. Next, the information needs of those business processes are identified and recorded in the dictionary and support the locating of data-sharing opportunities. All of this data — about business opportunities, processes, information, and sharing potential — can be made more manageable in the context of a data dictionary.

These planning processes are not yet fully realized at Company A. They depend on developing the DBA's own understanding of these methods and educating the corporate community in the advantages of the formal definitions of information entities.

Company A has thus embarked on a broad program for the management and control of its data resources.

7.4.5 Data Dictionary Use at Company B

Company B is a large telephone company in a large Canadian city. This company's data administration department has been evolving since 1977.

Company B has had the online IBM data dictionary for several years, but is not making extensive use of its capabilities. The data administration area uses the dictionary as a passive tool to maintain details of the database control blocks, database definitions, and the program specification blocks. The dictionary facilitates the management of several test and production versions of database definitions. The company has captured some descriptions of major databases and files and their fields, but has not progressed to the point of describing in detail all major databases and files.

The company reported that the IBM dictionary was not particularly user-friendly and has been relegated, almost solely, to use by the technical database support personnel. The company's information center personnel did not find the dictionary easy to use and found that the standard reports produced were somewhat lacking in user appeal. They found the screens used for input/query were not, however, easily changed and were definitely geared to more technical users than those which the information center supports.

7.4.6 Company B's Use of the Extensibility Feature of the Data Dictionary

The extensibility feature of the IBM data dictionary allows the user to code, debug, and document development systems and their programs. Entire batch or online transaction-driven systems can be developed using the extensibility features. However, Company B is not currently using these features.

The company is currently involved in the production of a corporate data model. Data administration is now considering placing the results of the data model into the extensibility categories in the dictionary, as the data model results are of prime importance to the management of data within the corporation.

Company B feels that no one dictionary on the market handles the areas of production control block and data definition program code, the data analysis byproducts, and the database design assistance requirements well enough to be the sole tool used in those areas. It is for these reasons that the data dictionary at Company B is not used extensively.

7.5   The Concept of Metadata

In order to manage data as a resource that is shared by users at levels in an organization, it is essential that data about data (metadata) be clearly specified, easily accessible, and well controlled. The first step in this process is to identify and describe those data objects that are of interest to the organization and about which the organization wishes to store information. The data used to identify and describe the objects is entered into the data dictionary system as metadata.

Metadata should not be confused with the user data or actual data that is stored in the dictionary. For example, the metadata for an attribute CUSTOMER NAME will describe the entry for that attribute as "the name of a person who conducts business with the organization," whereas the user data will give the name of the customer, e.g., "TOM CLARK."

An example of the metadata for an attribute in the data dictionary follows:

* ATTRIBUTE NAME — A symbolic or descriptive name conventionally used to identify the ATTRIBUTE and its representations. Attribute names are used as the preferred method of referencing ATTRIBUTES.
* ALIASES — A list of names used as alternate identifiers for the ATTRIBUTE and its representations.
* ATTRIBUTE DESCRIPTION — A free-form narrative containing a description of the ATTRIBUTE and its various representations.

The description contains a concise definition of the ATTRIBUTE in a form suitable for use in a glossary.

- ATTRIBUTE FUNCTION — A free-form narrative describing the corporate interest in the ATTRIBUTE and its physical representations. The narrative describes the purpose and use of the ATTRIBUTE as it relates to corporate objectives and the business functions used to achieve them.
- DEFINITION UPDATE SOURCE — A composite structure identifying the individuals or groups who updated a dictionary entry and the dates on which those updates were made. A single occurrence of the structure is recorded for each update. It takes the form

SOURCE (DATE)

where SOURCE is a 3-character field identifying the person or group who submitted the definition modification.

- DEFINITION ACCEPTANCE STATUS — A composite structure identifying the project teams or organizational groups who created the definition or who must be informed of its subsequent updates. The structure is used as the basis for propagating definition changes to support groups who may be affected by the proposed modifications.
- DEFINITION RESPONSIBILITY — A set of references to the organizational groups charged with the responsibility for the accuracy and ongoing integrity of a definition. The references are used to establish a relationship between the dictionary entry and the organizational groups identified as the definitive source of information about the ATTRIBUTE's meaning and use.
- STANDARD REPRESENTATION ENTRIES — A composite structure listing and physical characteristics of the representation defined to be the standard representation of ATTRIBUTE values.

Standard representation attributes are documented in the following form:

```
==  STANDARD REPRESENTATION ATTRIBUTES
    JUSTIFICATION           - LEFT
    CODING STRUCTURE        - ALPHABETIC
    DATA LENGTH             - 10 CHARACTERS
    UNITS OF MEASURE        - KILOMETER
    SCALE FACTOR            - 1000
    NUMERIC TYPE            - INTEGER
    NUMERIC PRECISION       - 6 DIGITS
    NUMERIC VALUE           - NEGATIVE
```

```
STORAGE FORMAT        - BINARY
RECORDING MODE        - FIXED
STORAGE LENGTH        - 3 BYTES
```

- ACCESS AUTHORITY — A set of references to the organizational groups within the company who have the right to grant access to ATTRIBUTE values.
- AUTHORIZED USERS — A set of references to the organizational groups who have been granted access privileges to the information represented by the ATTRIBUTE and its physical representations. The references identify who uses the ATTRIBUTE and whether or not they can create, delete, or modify ATTRIBUTE values.
- VALUE-SET ASSIGNMENT RESPONSIBILITY — A set of references to the organizational groups who have the right to add to, delete from, or otherwise modify the set of acceptable values which can be assumed by the ATTRIBUTE values.
- ENTITY CLASS MEMBERSHIP — A reference to the ENTITY CLASS, which includes the ATTRIBUTE as a component. The name must identify an ENTITY CLASS defined elsewhere in dictionary.
- LOGICAL GROUP MEMBERSHIP — A list of names identifying the LOGICAL GROUPS, which include the ATTRIBUTE as a component. The names in the list must correspond to the names associated with LOCAL GROUP DEFINITIONS recorded elsewhere in the dictionary.
- LOGICAL RECORD MEMBERSHIP — A list of names identifying the LOGICAL RECORDS containing physical representations of the ATTRIBUTE. The names included in the list must correspond to the names associated with LOGICAL RECORD DEFINITIONS recorded elsewhere in the dictionary.
- VALIDITY/EDIT RULES — A free-form narrative listing the edit rules which must be satisfied by ATTRIBUTE values stored in groups, segments, or similar physical data structures. The narrative includes, among others, syntactical rules dictating the format or internal structure of the ATTRIBUTE.
- CONSISTENCY CHECKS — A free-form narrative listing the consistency checks which must be satisfied by all ATTRIBUTE values. The narrative includes tables defining value correlations between related ATTRIBUTES.
- REASONABLENESS CHECKS — A narrative listing the reasonableness checks which, when applied against ATTRIBUTE values, identify values which are reasonable and should be further investigated. The narrative includes tables identifying acceptable subsets

of ATTRIBUTE values and the circumstances in which those restricted subsets apply.

- USAGE PROPAGATION — A free-form narrative describing the impact of changes made to ATTRIBUTE values held in physical data structures and the steps that must be taken to propagate the changes throughout the database.
- VALIDATION PROPAGATION — A free-form narrative describing the impact of changes to the set of acceptable values which can be assumed by an ATTRIBUTE, and the action necessary to update the acceptable values of other related ATTRIBUTES. The narrative includes the names of ATTRIBUTES whose acceptable values can be affected by the changes.

7.6   Contents of a Typical Data Dictionary

The typical data dictionary's contents can be generally classified into three groups: data contents, processing contents, and environment contents.

Data contents describe or represent dictionary entries that are units of data, for example, attributes, entities, segments, and databases.

Processing contents describe or represent dictionary entries that are processes, systems, programs, and transactions.

Environment contents describe or represent dictionary entries that are associated with the physical environment, for example, security features, users, terminals, and audit techniques.

7.6.1   The Data Dictionary as a Directory

"Data directory" is another term that is frequently used. As a rule, a dictionary gives the descriptions and definitions of an organization's data, whereas the directory gives the storage location of that data. However, many software vendors use these terms interchangeably, although some consistently use one or the other.

A data dictionary may contain a lot more than the location of stored data. It may be considered to be a machine-readable definition of computerized databases. It is often used by a database management system to obtain the sizes, formats, and locations of data records and fields. A data dictionary may be considered a superset that can contain additional data and definitions. Some vendors of database management systems now use the term "catalog" instead of "directory" or "dictionary." This usually means that the system includes a repository of metadata which is more extensive than the usual directory, but not as elaborate as a dictionary.

7.7   Maintenance of the Data Dictionary

The most important reason for the existence of a data dictionary is its ability to produce reports that are accurate and timely. For this reason, the maintenance of an organization's data dictionary is a very critical issue.

The maintenance of the data dictionary should be carried out in the following areas:

- Definitive information
- Propagation effects and control of changes
- Access authorization of users
- Consistency/validation checks
- Directory/data storage features
- Relationship/membership of entry
- Environmental data

The definitive information of the data dictionary will include the naming convention, the description and function of the entry, who is responsible for the definition and any subsequent update, and the data representation of the definition. Any maintenance carried out on the entries will ensure that the definitive information is correct and always reflects the current status in both accuracy and timeliness.

Any changes to the data dictionary contents should be made only after the effect of that change is evaluated. The person responsible for changes should determine which users, which programs and systems, and which relationships/cross-references will be affected. Ideally, all changes should be done from one central terminal or controlled by one central organization. Unauthorized or unapproved changes should never be allowed in the dictionary environment.

7.7.1   Access Authorization of Users

The data dictionary should always contain accurate and timely information on the access authorization of all users. This information should not only include access to the data dictionary itself, but also to the stored data. Any change in access authorization of a user should be immediately shown in the dictionary and appropriate measures taken to maintain the existing data security level.

7.7.2   Consistency/Validation Checks

Because of the multi-origin of names and definitions in the data dictionary, the number of inconsistencies in names is often great. Some organizations attempt to cut down on these cases by having several versions of the project data dictionary, and one dictionary designated as the corporate dictionary. Names and definitions are transferred to the corporate dictionary only when it is established that no changes will be made to the entry. Thus, the need for maintenance of the corporate dictionary, for this reason, seldom arises.

7.7.3   Directory/Data Storage Features

One function of the data dictionary is to act as a directory or pointer to the stored data or to the metadata. The dictionary may contain unique identifiers which will allow the user to determine the location of the metadata formats. For example, in a particular data dictionary developed in-house, the metadata was stored on seven volumes of disk storage. Each category of the definition carried an entry called "library identifier." This identifier took the form "XXXNNNNN," where 'XXX' was a 3-character alphabetic field identifying the volume containing the definition, and 'NNNNN' was a 5-character numeric field which served as a unique identifier within a volume.

A user wishing to access the dictionary definitions need only code the library identifier in the job control language (JCL) if running a batch mode or enter the Identifier when required to do so if running in an interactive mode.

7.7.4   Relationship/Membership of Entry

A very important feature of the data dictionary is its ability to show relationships between an attribute and the record to which it belongs, a file and its database, and a database and its logical schema. It is very important that these relationships are properly maintained. During update or deletion activities, these linkages must be maintained.

7.7.5   Environmental Data

Many data dictionaries contain entries describing the operating environment of the organization. For example, the entries may indicate whether a traditional operating environment or a database environment is used.

Other dictionaries may indicate the storage media for stored data or metadata. The maintenance aspect of data dictionaries must account for any change in the operating environment.

7.8   Active and Passive Dictionaries

Dictionaries are generally classified into two categories: passive and active.

In the passive mode, the dictionary is used mainly as a repository of information on attributes, records, files, databases, and schemas. A user wanting access to this information may go to a shelf and retrieve this information from the dictionary, or retrieve it from a computer if the dictionary is computerized.

In the active mode, the dictionary may be used in conjunction with the operating system to lock out unauthorized users from stored data or metadata. For example, the dictionary may contain an authorization table showing the names of users and the data they are authorized to access. A request from a user is channeled to the data dictionary and access authorization determined. If the request is legitimate, access to the data is granted. If the request exceeds the authorization, the request is denied and an audit trail for post facto analysis is created.

In an active mode, the data dictionary can be used for the automated design of databases. This feature is very often difficult to implement and may still be several years in the future for most organizations.

7.9   Design of Data Dictionaries

The next chapter will discuss in detail the design of data dictionaries. This section will serve to introduce the design of a basic data dictionary.

Data dictionaries are designed to give definite information about objects in which an organization may have an interest. The entries in the dictionary may include attributes, entities, records, files, and databases.

The typical entries for an attribute will include, among others, the name, any aliases, the description and function, data length, origin of definition of attribute, validity, update authorization, security, and consistency checks.

In addition to the above, the design should include features for accessing and retrieving from the dictionary.

7.10 Control and Audit Features of the Data Dictionary

The data dictionary can be used as a tool to control access to an organization's data. It can also be used by internal auditors to monitor the data security efforts of an organization.

In the area of controls, the data dictionary can be used to control changes to attributes, entities, or files. By including in the dictionary the names of those responsible for making changes, the organization can limit this activity to those authorized individuals.

The dictionary can also be used to control the effects that changes would have on users, programs, and applications. By including the names of those affected by changes, the organization can immediately notify those affected.

The dictionary can be used in both the active and passive modes to control access, not only to metadata but also to the stored data. An access-authorization table contained in the dictionary can be used to control access to data.

Internal auditors can use the data dictionary during systems development to ensure that agreed-upon standards are being adhered to by systems designers. They can use it to audit naming conventions and standards and to determine who are authorized users of the system and their authorization levels.

The data dictionary can be used in an active mode to interface with the operating system to produce audit trails to analyze attempts made by users to breach the organization's security.

7.11 Data Dictionary Standards

Data dictionary standards may fall into any of the following categories:

- Metadata contents
- Interface to external environment
- Interface with command languages
- Access rules and control
- Customized and management reports
- Security
- Interrelations between entries
- Extensibility

Standards in metadata contents would clearly indicate which entries should be found in the dictionary. For example, the standard entry for an attribute should include name, function, description, alias, definition responsibility, standard representation, edit rules, and access control features.

A dictionary design should include standards for interfacing with the external environment. In this regard, the standards may be as simple as including an entry describing the physical environment and its operating system, or as difficult as using the data dictionary to control access to the stored data and the operating system itself.

Standards for interfacing with command languages would indicate how high-level languages, such as Fortran and PL1, will use the data dictionary to build file structures and layouts, and how retrieval languages will access the data dictionary itself.

Standards for access rules and control would indicate who can access the dictionary, how the dictionary contents would be accessed, whether the contents would be accessed in its original form, or whether copies of the data would be accessed.

Standards in the area of security would cover the security of the data dictionary and its contents and security techniques for protecting the external environment.

Standards indicating the interrelations among entries would show how an attribute is related to a group, record, file, or database. In the reverse order, the standards should show what attributes comprise the database, entity, or file.

Standards in the area of extensibility would indicate what features can be included by the users and how the user can enhance the dictionary capability or make it more user-friendly.

7.12   Data Dictionary as a Tool for Data Analysis

Data analysis is defined as documenting the entities in which the organization has an interest. It is in this area that the data dictionary is most useful. In data analysis, the organization attempts to determine the entities and the role they play. The data dictionary can be used to record this information. The dictionary would give not only definitive information about the entities, but also the relationships between the entities and how these entities can be used to model the organization's data environment.

During the data analysis, inconsistencies, redundancies, and incompleteness in the data are determined. A source for such determinations is the data dictionary.

Again, during data analysis the development teams may want to determine the originators of the definition, whether the definition has homonyms or synonyms, and the aliases by which the definition may be identified. The dictionary should be the supplier of information to satisfy these queries.

Finally, the entries (metadata) in the data dictionary serve as a useful guideline or standard that can be followed by the data analyst who wishes to document information about attributes, entities, and relationships in an efficient and structured manner.

8

The Data Dictionary in Systems Design

Introduction

The role of the data dictionary in the design, implementation, and maintenance of database systems has been well documented. The growing awareness of data as a corporate resource, resulting in data-driven, rather than process-driven systems, has led to recognition of the impact of data on departments outside of data processing. In this way, the system development life cycle has developed from a point where the focus of concern was on highly localized data processing problems. It is now recognized that the efficiency of a given system usually depends upon its end-user orientation, and how well it represents and serves the organization as a whole. Current methodologies are becoming less process-oriented and more data-oriented.

It is because of this new awareness that the data dictionary can play a significant part in supporting the SDLC. It provides a wealth of detail upon which early research work can be based and is then an invaluable communications tool between the different departments involved in the SDLC.

It is for these reasons that the succeeding sections discuss the role of the data dictionary in the SDLC.

8.1   What is a Data Dictionary?

Data dictionary can be defined as an organized reference to the data content of an organization's programs, systems, databases, collections of all files, or manual records. The data dictionary may be maintained manually or by computer. Sometimes the term "data dictionary" refers specifically to a software product that is utilized to maintain a dictionary database. The data dictionary will contain names, descriptions, and definitions of the organization's data resources.

8.2   The Concept of Metadata

In the broadest sense, a data dictionary is any organized collection of information about data. In the real world, any information system, whether or not it is computerized, exists to store and process data about objects (entities). We then create data records to represent occurrences of these entities. We define specific record types to represent specific entity types. Frequently we also assign keys or identifiers, such as customer names and invoice numbers, to differentiate one record occurrence from another. A data dictionary can then be designed that contains data about those customer and invoice record types.

The customer and invoice records in the database contain ordinary data. The records in the database contain ordinary data. The record in the data dictionary contains metadata, or data about the data. For example, the record in the data dictionary may contain the name, the record length, the data characteristics, and the recording mode of the record in the database.

8.3   Active vs. Passive Data Dictionaries

Data dictionaries are often categorized as active or passive. This refers to the extent of their integration with the database management system. If the data dictionary and the DBMS are integrated to the extent that the DBMS uses the definitions in the dictionary at run time, the dictionary is active. If the dictionary is freestanding or independent of the DBMS, it is passive.

An active dictionary must contain an accurate, up-to-date description of the physical database in order for the database management

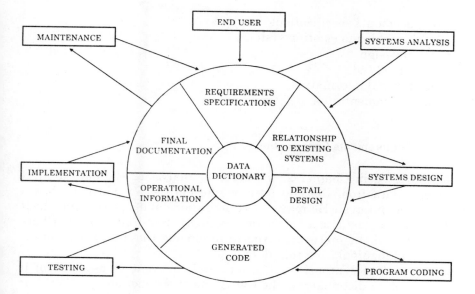

Figure 8-1 The SDLC Showing the Data Dictionary as a Communication and Documentation Tool

system to access the data. In a passive dictionary environment, more effort is required to keep two copies of the same data, and great care must be taken to ensure that the two copies are actually identical.

8.4 The Role of the Data Dictionary in the SDLC

The role of the data dictionary in the system development life cycle is shown in Figure 8-1.

Any analysis of the figure will show that the data dictionary is at the core of systems design and development. The metadata collected in the dictionary about the different phases of the SDLC are demonstrated in the second layer of the diagram. The third layer depicts the various interfaces to the different phases of the SDLC. The directions of the arrows indicate that the interfaces act as input to the phases and also extract design information from the phases.

As we move in a clockwise direction around the second layer, we notice, starting with the input from the end users, that the following types of metadata are collected:

- Requirements specifications
- Relationships to existing systems
- Detail design
- Generated code
- Operational information
- Final documentation

8.4.1 Requirements Specifications

As indicated in Chapter 2, the systems analyst or the data analyst collects data from the end user on the entities in which he has a particular interest. He may collect definitions and descriptions about the entities, data characteristics, security requirements, attribute content, and the processes involved in moving the data across interfaces and manipulating that data.

The analyst synthesizes this data and then enters as much of it into the data dictionary as the constructs of the dictionary allow. For example, in the DATAMANAGER data dictionary marketed by Manager Software Products (MSP), the analyst can enter data about the system, file, groups of data, and data items that will constitute a solution to the user's requirements.

8.4.2 Relationship to Existing Systems

In arriving at what may be the optimum solution to the user's requirements, the analyst must seek to determine from the dictionary:

- If a system already exists that can solve the problem.
- If no system exists, what portions of the existing systems can be used in his solution.
- If alternate solutions can be obtained.

8.4.3 Detail Design

During detail system design, the analyst will enter data about the data models, the process flows, the programming specifications, the file layouts, and report formats. If the current design has any relationship to designs already existing in the data dictionary, the analyst can extract that portion and implement it with the new metadata.

8.4.4   Generated Code

The data dictionary contains copy books (source statements) and source statements or pointers to source statement libraries that may be extracted for use in program testing.

It is now possible to generate code from process definitions and programming specifications stored in the data dictionary. Current CASE tools can generate this code for several languages and several different platforms; e.g., PC or mainframe.

8.4.5   Operational Information

The data dictionary may contain information that will enable the data processing staff to execute the programs. This information may include run instructions, job control language (JCL) setup, distribution information, test plans and requirements, and processing exceptions.

8.4.6   Final Documentation

The final documentation information stored in the data dictionary may include user-manual instructions, impact analysis information, acceptance testing and sign-off information, change control information, and job control language information.

8.5   Interfaces to the Data Dictionary

Interfaces to the data dictionary are many and varied. They act in two directions: the deliverables to the dictionary and from the dictionary. These interfaces include:

- End user
- Systems analysis
- Systems design
- Program coding
- Testing
- Implementation
- Maintenance

8.5.1   The End User

The end user is the primary source of input to the requirements specifications phase of systems development. It is during this phase that data is collected on the objectives and scope of the project, the data and processing requirements, the operating environment, alternative processing, data security, and the input and output formats.

The advent of database management systems, structured design methodologies, and new development tools has signaled a larger role for the end user in systems development. The end user is as much a part of the systems development team as the data analyst or systems analyst. The success or failure of the system depends, to a large degree, on the quality of the data collected on the user requirements.

8.5.2   The Systems Analysis Phase

During the systems analysis phase, data is obtained from the end user and the user requirements specifications and fed into the systems design phase. The relationship to existing systems data is stored in the data dictionary.

During this phase, the data and systems analyst will iteratively extract data from the requirements specifications already stored in the data dictionary, augment it with that from the end user and any obtained from existing systems to come up with data and process models which form the primary deliverables of the systems design phase.

If, during the systems analysis phase, no data is found in the data dictionary that connects the current system with other systems, the analyst enters any existing relationships into the data dictionary.

8.5.3   The Systems Design Phase

During the systems design phase, the data analyst extracts information from the analysis phase and relationship to existing systems stored in the data dictionary and develops a data model. This model is, in turn, stored in the data dictionary as detail design metadata. Meanwhile, the systems (process) analyst develops a process model with information from the data dictionary and the systems analysis phase. The data collected during this phase is stored in the detail design section of the data dictionary and used as input, through programming specifications, to the program coding phase.

8.5.4   The Program Coding Phase

During the program coding phase, the programmer/analyst takes specifications from the systems design phase and couples it with metadata from the detail design information stored in the data dictionary to produce program code for the testing phase and to be stored as metadata and sometimes source data in the data dictionary.

8.5.5   The Testing Phase

During this phase, the analysts take program code from the program coding phase and generated code stored in the data dictionary and tests it, to obtain operational metadata to be stored in the data dictionary and program code for the implementation phase.

8.5.6   The Implementation Phase

During this phase, operational information metadata stored in the data dictionary is coupled with the tested program code to produce implementable systems. The results from this phase are stored in the data dictionary as a final document and are used as input to the maintenance phase.

8.5.7   The Maintenance Phase

During this phase, metadata from the final document stored in the data dictionary and input from the implementation phase are used to maintain the production systems. This phase also encompasses the updating of requirements specifications stored in the data dictionary and the constant reporting to the user of the results of these changes.

8.6   The Data Dictionary as a Documentation Tool

As mentioned earlier, the data dictionary plays a significant role in the systems development life cycle. One major role is documenting the results of each phase of the SDLC. This section describes some of the entries that are documented in the data dictionary for the major phases of the SDLC.

8.6.1   Documenting the System Design Phase

The data dictionary can offer substantial assistance to the designer during the system design phase by providing the source and storage of the inputs and outputs of the design step. The inputs to data design are full descriptions of the business processes and the data required by these processes. The outputs are the logical views and the logical database (also known as logical schemes). A logical database refers to a structuring of entities and relations between entities supporting the business processes of the application.

There are many different methods of transforming the business processes and their required data into a logical database. One is a top-down data design method identifying entities and the relationships between the entities before defining the attributes of each entity.

Alternatively, there are bottom-up data design techniques, which encourage the description of entities, and the attributes identifying the entities, before identifying relationships between entities.

There are five basic steps in top-down data design:

• Identifying the business functions of the application.
• Identifying the data required by each function and the procedure by which data is collected.
• Identifying the entities of the application.
• Defining the relationships between the entities.
• Ascribing attributes to their entities.

Nowhere is the importance of the data dictionary more obvious than it is in the building of the function's logical model. As the keeper of the "who," "what," and "how" of the organizational information system, the data dictionary provides full descriptions of:

• The business functions
• The data generated by and used by the business functions
• The application entities
• The relationships of the application's entities to one another
• The attributes of the entities

Frequently, data itself goes through an evolutionary process, its definition becoming more and more refined until it can finally be set. Data also can be perceived simultaneously from several user points of view. A data dictionary that has facilities for multiple logical dictionaries can document the history of a data item or process as well as hold these varied points of view. This can be a most valuable aid during the design stage.

8.6.2   Documenting the Detailed Design Phase

In a business system plan (BSP) the design phase is comprised of two levels, the general design and the detailed design, in which business activities, data, entities, relationships and attributes are described, not just on the application level, but from a higher level providing a corporate, transfunctional perspective. In BSP, the methodology is the same as with SDLC; it is simply engineered on a higher plane. Once these elements are plugged in, they remain in documented form on the data dictionary and can be accessed for future systems development as well. Another feature of the data dictionary that can prove to be most useful at this point in the SDLC is its facility for providing implicit as well as explicit relationships. The systems designer, who might otherwise overlook these implicit relationships, is spared one more trap to fall into.

8.6.3   Documenting the Physical Design Phase

The details of physical design depend very much on the characteristics of the DBMS chosen for the database design.
   In an IMS environment, the physical design includes the following selections:

• Physical databases and types of logical relationships, whether unidirectionally or bidirectionally physically paired
• Access methods, whether HISAM, HIDAM, or HDAM
• Segments and hierarchical structures and data representation, including type and size
• Secondary indices
• Types of pointers in relationships

   The data dictionary is a very useful tool to document these selections. In addition, volume and usage statistics necessary for the ordering of database segments and for determination of storage estimates can be documented in the data dictionary.

8.6.4   Documenting the Implementation Phase

The implementation phase is very often not considered a part of the SDLC because by that point, the system has been installed and consequently has entered a separate, operational period.

It is a stage that has enormous impact on not just the system, but the entire organization. Maintenance is also a task especially well served by the data dictionary, which can provide:

- Complete up-to-date documentation of the system
- An historical and multiuser perspective view of the development of the definitions of the systems entities, process entities, and the relationships among them
- Enforcement of the use of definitions in a logical manner
- Security of the integrity of these definitions
- The means of assessing the impact of system changes

Consequently, the maintenance staff is provided with a comprehensive and logically consistent picture of the system, its functions, processes, and data components. They are thus properly prepared to respond to changes in needs in ways which will minimize error and save time, money and frustration.

The maintenance stage is also the point at which the use of the data dictionary as a systems development tool is most easily validated. Systems founded upon data dictionary resources are most likely to be spared the unnecessary and yet most typical function of maintenance, rectification of bad systems planning and specifications. Consequently, they are the ones most likely to free the maintenance stage for its proper function of adapting the system to the organization's changing environment. Obviously, this frees up the staff for the development of new systems and reduces many of the external pressures otherwise imposed on all systems.

8.6.5   Documenting the Structured Maintenance Phase

Structured maintenance deals with the procedures and guidelines to achieve system change or evolution through the definition of data structure change to accommodate the requirements of system change. The inputs to structured maintenance are user change requests and the current system, including database design and systems design. These are included in the data dictionary. The output from structured maintenance is, ideally, a system reflecting the user change request.

There are five steps in structured maintenance:

- Identify the changes to the data structures required to accommodate the user request.
- Identify the program functions which currently process the data structures. These program functions are reviewed and systems changes are identified.
- Determine the cost of the change. One of the benefits of this method is that it quickly indicates significant costly changes, seen when the data structures required to accommodate the change are very different from the current data structures.
- Perform the implementation — if the cost is acceptable.
- Test the results.

Structured maintenance thus goes through all of the steps of the structured system development methodology as defined here.

This is an effective way to minimize the need to recover from past mistakes of the system, whether they are the result of unstructured or structured methodologies.

A system development life cycle is used to produce the means by which the organizational data is to be manipulated. Before it may be manipulated, however, it must be managed, and that is the function of the data dictionary.

8.7   The Data Dictionary and Data Security

In the database environment, the data dictionary can be used to protect the organization's data. Entries may indicate who has access rights to what data and who can update or alter that data. It can also be used to indicate who has responsibility for creating and changing definitions.

Current data dictionaries utilize several different protection mechanisms to effect data security in an environment. Also, data dictionaries can have pointers in an "AUTHORIZATION" section to various data security software packages. Some of these are:

- Access management
- Privacy transformations
- Cryptographic controls
- Security kernels
- Access matrix

Due to space constraints, I will not discuss all of these mechanisms at length, but will instead refer you to some of the current literature on data security.

8.7.1   Access Management

These techniques are aimed at preventing unauthorized users from obtaining services from the system or gaining access to its files. The procedures involved are authorization, identification, and authentication. Authorization is given for certain types of information. Users attempting to enter the system must first identify themselves and their locations and then authenticate the identification.

8.7.2   Privacy Transformations

Privacy transformations are techniques for concealing information by coding the data in user-processor communications or in files. Privacy transformations consist of sets of logical operations on the individual characters of the data. Privacy transformations break down into two general types: irreversible and reversible. Irreversible privacy transformations include aggregation and random modification. In this case, valid statistics can be obtained from such data, but individual values cannot be.

Reversible privacy transformations are as follows:

- Coding — Replacement of a group of words in one language by a word in another language.
- Compression — Removal of redundancies and blanks from transmitted data.
- Substitution — Replacement of letters in one or more items.
- Transposition — Distortion of the sequence of letters in the ciphered text; all letters in the original text are retained in this technique.
- Composite transformation — Combinations of the above methods.

8.7.3   Cryptographic Controls

Cryptographic transformations were recognized long ago as an effective protection mechanism in communication systems. In the past, they were used mainly to protect information transferred through communication lines.

There is still much debate about the cost/benefit ratio of encrypting large databases. My experience with encryption indicates that the cost of producing clear text from large encrypted databases is prohibitive.

8.7.4 Security Kernels

Security kernels, as the name suggests, are extra layers of protection surrounding operating systems. The kernels are usually software programs used to test for authenticity and to either authorize or deny all user requests to the operating system.

A request to the operating system to execute a task or retrieve data from the database is routed to the security kernel, where the request is examined to determine if the user is authorized to access the requested data. If all checks are passed, the request is transmitted to the operating system, which then executes the request.

8.8 Data Dictionary Standards

There are two types of data-related standards for data dictionaries: data definition standards and data format conformance.

"Data definition" refers to a standard way of describing data. One example is the naming of data. The naming standard may be in the form of rigid rules or established conventions for assigning names to data entities.

All user areas within the enterprise will know that, for instance, the data element "customer name" — used in files, programs and reports — means the same throughout the enterprise.

"Data format conformance" is content-related. It means that a data element, in addition to having the same name throughout the enterprise, also must conform to a common set of format rules for the data element to retain the same meaning. For example, all data elements involving "data" should have the same format throughout the enterprise — and only that format should be assigned. Similarly, if codes are to be used throughout the enterprise, they must be uniform. If an acceptable "state" code is two letters, that must be the universally accepted code in the enterprise, and no other code, whether one, three, or four letters, should be used.

8.8.1   Standard Formats for Data Dictionary Entries

Standards are required for the format and content used in defining and describing metaentities of the data dictionary. This means setting standards for the type of information that must be collected for each entry type and, most important, for the conventions that must be observed in defining these attributes. In effect, this amounts to defining a set of standards for methods of preparing attribute, entity, and relationship descriptions.

There are a number of general guidelines for establishing a standard. Several standard entries are available in commercially produced dictionaries. However, a typical standard entry for a data element is shown in Figure 8-2. A data element may be described in terms of the attributes in this figure.

8.8.2   Standards for Programs Interfacing with a Data Dictionary

Data dictionary standards for programming interfaces basically fall into the area of the structure of the "call" statement from the programming language to the dictionary package.

Data Element	Definition
Identification number	A 7-character unique identifier beginning with ELXXXXX
Designator	A short name composed of the keywords of the DESCRIPTION
Programming name	An abbreviated form of the DESIGNATOR using only approved abbreviations. Example: LEGL-CUST-NAME
Description	A narrative explanation of the data element; the first sentence must identify the real-world entity being described. The second sentence may expand on usage characteristics. Example: The name of a customer, which is the legal name. It may not be the commonly used name. It is usually derived from legal papers.

Figure 8-2   Sample Standard for Data Element Description

Other standards in this area will indicate how high-level languages will use the data dictionary to build file structures and record layouts from "COPY" books. They will also indicate how these languages will access the dictionary itself.

8.8.3   Security Standards

Standards for access rules and controls will indicate who can access the dictionary, how the dictionary will be accessed, and whether the contents will be accessed in their original form or as copies.

Standards in the area of security will cover the use of the data dictionary as a protection mechanism and the entries that must be made in the data dictionary to achieve those standards.

8.9   Examples of Data Dictionary Entries

There are several commercially available data dictionaries, each with its own metadata entries and standards. This section illustrates entries for three available dictionaries:

- Xerox Data Dictionary (XDD)
- MSP Datamanager
- IBM DB/DC

8.9.1   The Xerox Data Dictionary

Functional requirements — The dictionary software must process certain essential features to properly support the Xerox administrative and data processing environment, including:

- Local users and data administrators in controlling their data processing environment
- Multinational systems designers and users
- Technical designers and programmers in implementing and maintaining systems on a local and multinational level
- Audit, security, and systems control needs of Xerox management

These functions can be divided as follows:

- Data Definitions

  1. Describe data elements
  2. Describe physical and logical records
  3. Allow for mechanical generation of entity code or name
  4. Relate elements and records to program and modules

- Data Administration:

  1. Support data element definition
  2. Describe usage of standards and procedures in programs, systems, and data entries
  3. Relate entity definitions to authorized owners
  4. Rename dictionary entities

- System and Program Definition and Support:

  1. Describe programs
  2. Provide for description of functional interfaces
  3. Relate a program (module) to other programs (modules) that call and are called by the program (module)
  4. Describe and generate online screen formatting characteristics

- User Access:

  1. Cross-referencing of all dictionary-defined entities
  2. Access to any dictionary-defined entity by its generic name, entity code, or ALIAS
  3. "Where used" reporting for all entities-single and full level
  4. COPY and MACRO library member generation
  5. Online access for inquiry and update

- Database Definition Administration:

  1. Describe databases (one definition per database)
  2. Relate databases to their components and to program
  3. Relate databases to elements
  4. Generate mechanically as data definitions and relationships for database development (e.g., DBDs, PSBs, etc.)
  5. Provide interface for external entity editing control for dictionary transactions

- Data Dictionary:

  1. All organizations involved in data definitions and usage will maintain records describing the data entities and usage and relationship
  2. Corporate data naming standards and attribute definitions will be followed for all mechanized data dictionaries
  3. All information systems organizations should establish migration strategies to Xerox Data Dictionary for all operational systems

- Data Element Attributes:

  1. Element name — Specifies the descriptive name of the data element
  2. Element description — Provides narrative text/description of the data element
  3. Element length — Specifies the number of positions required for one occurrence of the data element as entered
  4. Element format — Specifies the character category of the element, such as numeric, alphabetic
  5. Responsibility — Specifies the organization or function responsible for the data element definition

- Security:

  1. Registered
  2. Private
  3. Unclassified
  4. Personal

- Status:

  1. Draft — Applies to data entered into the dictionary for the purpose of facilitating the early system design process
  2. Proposed — A user using the dictionary proposes an addition, deletion, or change to meet a system's requirement
  3. Approved — When testing is completed to the satisfaction of the administrator, the specification's status is changed to "approved"
  4. Active — Indicates the entity is being used in a productive system

- Synonym — Specifies a data element as having nearly the same name and/or meaning as another element
- Coding/Edit Rules — Indicates coding structures, conventions, composition, and any special edit rules
- Data Dictionary Naming Standard:

1. Primary Name —Primary names for elements and groups will be descriptive English, not exceeding 32 characters
2. Higher-level entities — No classword is required on items or groups, but for higher-level entities a leading classword is to be used, such as SYS-XXXX

8.9.2   MSP Datamanager

The MSP Datamanager is a data dictionary marketed by Manager Software Products (MSP).

It has the following basic structure:

- System
- Program
- Module
- File
- Group
- Data item

The data structure is useful to both user and data dictionary in terms of establishing data relationships and the levels of importance of each of the above member types.

8.9.3   Discussion of Member Types

- System — The highest level of the member type hierarchy. They can be subsystems to other systems. They can be declaration of the programs, modules, files, groups, and data items processed in the system.
- Program — Contains or calls other programs and/or modules, inputs, outputs or updates files, groups and/or data items.
- Module — An independent set of instructions. May be used by other programs.
- File — May be manual or automated. Contains records. Its records contain groups and/or data items. May also contain other files.

- Group — A combination of data items and/or other groups. May be an entire record or a subset of data items found on a record. May be used to describe information on a preprinted form.
- Data item — The fundamental element of data. Smallest name unit into which data is divided in the user organization.

8.9.4   Entries in Datamanager

- System

Effective Date	'10-9-95'
Obsolete Date	'12-31-99'
Alias	'MGA'
Contains	'MGA03001-XTRACT-IPMF'
	'MGA03002-CREATE-IPMF'
	'MGA03003-SELECT-IPMF'
	'MGA03003-CREATE-UPD'
	'MGA03004-TAG-PURGED'
Frequency Run	'Weekly'.
Catalog	'System'
	'batch'
Catalog-owner	'Annette Green'
Note	'Year in Production-1988'
Administrative-Data	'Application Narrative'
Project ID:	'Project ID. MGAP'
Prepared By: Freida Roxax	Date: 10/19/88

A. System Objective

   To function as an interface between Cycare-based Medical Group systems and the new IPMF update processing.

B. System Functions

   1. Reformat IPMF and transmittal tapes for subsequent processing.
   2. Generate a summary of all changes done on a particular policy.

3. Provide a copy of all updating transactions to all Cycare-based Medical Center, properly flagged according to changes undergone by each policy.

C. System Features
MGA uses inputs from the registration and capitation systems.

8.9.5   The IBM DB/DC Data Dictionary

The DB/DC data dictionary is comprised of a set of databases that are used to store and access information about an installation's data processing resources.

The dictionary contains data about data.

Subject Categories

• IBM-defined

— Systems/subsystems
— Jobs
— Programs/modules
— Databases
— PSBs/PCBs
— Segments/records
— Data elements

• Installation-defined

— Business function
— Logical transactions
— Data classes
— Physical transactions
— Reports
— OS files
— Reusable packets

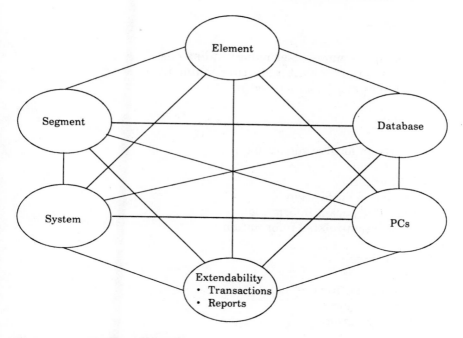

Figure 8-3   Dictionary Databases

Information on Subjects

• Name

    — Unique/meaningful
    — Primary/alias
    — 1 to 31 positions/language (BAL/Cobol/PL/I)

• Attributes

    — Depends on category
    — Language of program
    — Length of a data element

- Description

  — Descriptive name (user name) on line one
  — Any descriptive matter starting on line three
  — 999 lines of 72 positions each

- User data

  — Provision for five separate types
  — Audit trail
  — Edit criteria
  — System identification
  — Reusable packet information
  — Application-related information

- Relationships

  — To other entities
  — System to job
  — Job to program

- Relationship data

  — Information about the relationship between two entities
  — Indicative key (data element within segment)

Identification of Subjects (Dictionary Name)

- Components of name

  — Status code
    Identifies status of entity
  — Subject category (code)
    Identifies category
  — Name
    Primary name on the dictionary
  — Occurrences
    Distinguishes different physical attributes

- All the identifiers are required while working with a subject (subject name)

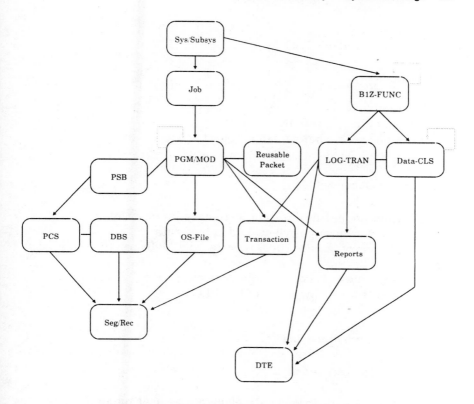

Figure 8-4 Data Dictionary Relationship Diagram

Accessing the Dictionary

- Interactive online facility

  — Screens for each subject
  — Prompting for action
  — Screen-to-screen access
  — Available through TSO terminals
  — Used for entry/update/retrieval

- Batch forms

  — Card image
  — Identifying control information on each record
  — Bulk data processing

— For entering only
— Available through TSO

• Commands

— Interactive online
— Within batch processing
— Example: scan, change name, report

Procedure for Documentation

• Application group fills out data dictionary input forms
• Data dictionary group reviews and enters data
• Data dictionary group runs reports and delivers to application group
• Input forms may also be used for corrections
• Order of entities follow order of the PLC

Data Element Entry Procedure

• Application project team

— Identifies and describes data elements by user name

• Supplies data element I/P forms to data dictionary administration
• Data dictionary administration

— Assigns descriptors
— Performs redundancy analysis
— Develops Cobol names
— Assigns BAL name
— Enters data elements in dictionary
— Sends data elements and cross reference report to application project team

8.10   Summary

This chapter discussed the role of the data dictionary in the development of systems in a database environment. It indicated what inputs

Table 8-1   Entry of Information into Data Dictionary

Project life cycle	Database design	Data dictionary documentation
Feasibility	Conceptual design	System/subsystems business functions data classes
Functional analysis	Detailed conceptual design	Logical transactions data elements reports
System design	Logical DB design	Segments Jobs Program/modules Reusable packets OS files Physical transactions
Implementation	Physical DB design	Databases PSBs/PCBs

and outputs the dictionary generated for each phase and the interface with the relevant phase personnel.

The chapter closed with a summary of the structure of three data dictionaries. The last two are very successful and widely used.

The author would like to refer his readers to a detailed coverage of data dictionaries discussed in his book *Analysis, Design, and Implementation of Data Dictionaries.*

9

Business Systems Planning — Strategic Data Planning

Introduction

Although information systems may provide intended results, many companies give little thought to the potential value of serving overall corporate objectives with systems capable of sharing data among executives and departments. Piecemeal systems development leaves many organizations with numerous nonintegrated, inflexible information systems. Nor has thought been given to the information needed to support managerial decision making and strategic planning; instead, the purpose of most of today's automated information systems is to enhance operational control or transaction-processing activities.

It has been estimated that the typical organization without a corporatewide data model spends approximately 80 percent of each systems development dollar to restructure existing application programs and data files to keep up with changing information needs. Also, an organization may be depriving itself of a major competitive advantage if it fails to manage its information-processing resources efficiently and creatively.

The best way to avoid the problems associated with the traditional approach to developing information systems is to adopt a formal systems planning methodology. This is a predetermined process by which the senior executives in an organization supply input that can be used to translate the organization's strategic goals into a detailed information systems development plan for achieving those goals. The next several sections of this chapter discuss such a plan.

9.1   The Business Systems Plan

The Business Systems Plan (BSP) was first made available to customers in 1970. BSP is defined as a structured approach to assist an organization in establishing an information systems plan to satisfy its short- and long-term information needs. BSP is a way to translate business strategy into information systems strategy.

Some objectives of BSP include:

* Impartially determining information systems priorities
* Planning long-lived information systems based on enduring business processes
* Managing systems resources to support business goals
* Assigning systems resources to high-return projects
* Improving user department and information systems department relations
* Improving understanding of the need to plan information systems

The BSP methodology's major premise is that organizationwide information systems should be planned from the top down and implemented piece by piece from the bottom up. Top-down planning means that a group of top executives provides a study consisting of managers, professionals, and information systems experts with the broad strategic objectives of an organization, as well as other important information. The study team systematically composes them into an architecture of information systems that will support the organization's strategy.

The BSP methodology consists of five major activities:

* Developing the BSP
* Documenting the business objective
* Defining the business entities
* Defining the information architecture
* Reporting the finding to management

9.2   Developing the BSP

The most important activity of the BSP is to develop a plan for conducting the BSP study. The plan should cover what the objectives of the study are, how the study will be conducted, who will participate in the study, and the expected deliverables from the study. A typical plan will contain the following:

* Goals of the study
* Scope of the study
* Problems addressed by the study
* What the study will do for the organization
* Deliverables from the study
* The study team
* The interviewees
* The timetable

9.2.1   Goals of the Study

The goals of the study are broad statements indicating what will be accomplished by undertaking the study. For example, the defined goals of the BSP study could be as follows:

* Establish an MIS Systems Plan which will be synchronized with and in support of the organization's business goals and strategies
* Provide an overall data architecture and application system architecture for the organization
* Provide system implementation strategies
* Provide action plans and resources requirements for the implementation strategies

9.2.2   Scope of the Study

The scope of the study sets the boundaries for the study. It indicates what will or will not be included in the study. For example, for an organization located in one area, the scope may indicate what departments of that organization will or will not be included in the study. For an organization spread over several geographically diverse areas, the scope may indicate that only the head office and not the branch offices will be included in the study.

9.2.3   Problems Addressed by the Study

This section of the plan establishes the reasons for conducting the study. It details problems that currently exist in the MIS area of the organization. Although existing problems are highlighted, no solutions are offered at this time. Some of the problems that may be highlighted for an organization are as follows:

• MIS projects experience cost and/or schedule overruns
• Complaints are often made about the quality, timeliness, and effectiveness of MIS service
• Application systems are not congruent with the organization's business goals and are brought into line only with great difficulty and expense
• Senior management feels that MIS is not effectively under its control. It cannot understand why projects:

— Are so big
— Take so long
— Require such large staff
— Are so expensive

• Maintenance projects are using almost 80 percent of the manpower
• Many application systems are old and out of date; they do not meet current company needs
• New products cannot be easily added to the organization's systems

9.2.4   What the Study Will Do for the Organization

This section of the plan further strengthens the objectives of the study and identifies some of the tangible results of the study. Some of these results are as follows:

• BSP will provide identification of business opportunities for employing information technologies
• BSP will provide a data architecture which constrains the design and development of new information systems so that all information systems will be consistent with one another
• BSP will provide a framework within which trade-off decisions can be made between short-term investments and long-term ones

- BSP supports companywide top-down systems design, but will allow for bottom-up, piece-by-piece implementation that will be made necessary by the realities of budget constraints, limited resources, and the drive for short-term results.

9.2.5   Deliverables from the Study

The main deliverables from the study will be a comprehensive report which will detail an overall data architecture and application system architecture for the organization, system implementation strategies, and action plans and resource requirements for the implementation strategies.

9.2.6   The Study Team and Interviewees

The composition of the study team is critical to the success of the study. The team should be made up of high-level management, preferably from the vice-president level; users, at the department head level; and senior MIS personnel.

The interviewees should be senior executives who are knowledgeable about the mission, goals, and objectives of the organization. They should be personnel with ranking no lower than the vice-president level.

9.3   Conducting the BSP Study

There are approximately 13 major steps to perform in conducting a BSP study. Two of them — gaining executive commitment and preparing for the study — precede the study itself. All of the steps are important; although some can be carried out to varying degrees, none can be completely eliminated. The following sections summarize the steps and their significance for senior executives.

9.3.1   Gaining Executive Commitment

A BSP study must not begin without a commitment from a top executive sponsor. In addition, other executives must be willing to become involved in it. Success depends on the degree to which these executives can supply the study team with other views of the organization and its data needs.

A key part of this first step is the concurrence of all parties regarding the effort's purpose and scope. Differing expectations are common and can lead to disappointing results and unmet expectations. Furthermore, the purpose of the study is to commit the organization to a course of action based on recommendation made at the study's end; therefore, early expectations are critical.

The choice of the team leader follows. The team leader may or may not be the executive sponsor: in some cases, the sponsor feels comfortable leading the study, but in others, a different manager is more appropriate. The team leader will direct the study team full time for the six to eight weeks the team typically requires. A team of four to seven members is recommended. The leader must be in a position to ensure that the team members have access to other important executives and must properly interpret members' thoughts and ideas.

The team members must be prepared to "sell" the study to executive sponsors and the interviewees. The "selling" effort must address:

• The purpose and scope of the study
• Some of the problems that will be addressed by the study
• What the study will do for the organization
• The identification of the team members who will work on the study
• The identification of those who will be interviewed
• The time commitment required of each executive

9.3.2   Preparing for the Study

Everyone should know the BSP plans and procedures before the study is conducted so that executives provide optional input and the study team can make optional use of the input. Study team interviewees should be identified as soon as possible so that their interviews can be scheduled. Information on the organization's basic business functions and its current data processing configuration should be compiled during this phase to facilitate the team training and orientation. The team should be given exclusive use of a conveniently located control room where study activities can be conducted. By the end of this phase, the team should produce a study control book containing:

• A study work plan
• List of executives to be interviewed and interview schedule

- A schedule for reviews with the executive sponsor at certain check-points
- Outline of final report
- Business and information systems data: analyzed, charted, and ready for use in the study

The executive sponsor should review the accomplishments made during this phase before actually beginning the study.

9.3.3 Starting the Study

The BSP study begins with three presentations to the study team:

- The executive sponsor repeats the purpose of the study and its anticipated output
- The team leader reviews business facts already collected so that each team member is thoroughly up to date.
- The senior information systems executive discusses the department's recent activities and problems so that the study team members understand its current role in the organization.

9.3.4 The Enterprise Analysis

This is the most important phase of the BSP study. Here, the study team identifies the current and accurate organization structure; the business strategies that exist to enable the organization to achieve its mission, goals, and objectives; the business processes or logically related decisions and activities that are required to manage the resources of the business; and the data classes or entities. This step is important because failure to define the strategies and processes properly will be reflected in all that follows.

9.3.5 Define Business Strategies

Business strategies are provided by the executive management team. The target output from this step should be a list of four to eight goals and approximately five strategies per goal. A sample list of strategies is as follows:

- Improve inventory control
- Streamline customer order cycle
- Tie production schedule closer to customer demand
- Manage inventories centrally
- Reduce losses due to bad debts
- Reduce raw material expenses by supplier agreements
- Increase advertising penetration
- Expand selling relationships with major department stores

The study team may expand these strategies to a form that will produce the major processes for the study. For example, the strategy "improve inventory control" may be expanded to read "develop a more comprehensive system for tracking information as to what items are located in each warehouse and where they are within the warehouse."

The next step in this phase is to produce a "strategy vs. organization" matrix. An example of such a matrix is shown in Figure 9-1.

Strategy \ Organization	Product Dev	Manufact'g	Ware./Dist.	Sales	Advertising	Contrlr
Improv Inv Cntrl		X	●	/		/
Strm Order Cycle			X	●		
Expand Prod Line	●	/		X		X
Inc Adv Penetratn				X	●	X
Central Inv Mgmt		X	●	/		/
Supplr Agreemnts	X	●				X

● Primary responsibility
X Major involvement
/ Minor involvement

Figure 9-1 Strategy vs. Organization Matrix

9.3.6   Define Business Processes

Business processes may be defined as a group of logically related decisions and activities significant to the enterprise. During this phase, the study team seeks to define a set of processes that are in place in the organization. The target output from this step is a list of 40–60 business processes. The criteria for selecting these processes are that the process should be:

- Independent of organizational structure
- Significant to the enterprise
- Named by verb-object
- Nonredundant activities and decisions
- Able to be aggregated or disaggregated
- Unique for each enterprise

The study team develops a "process vs. organization" matrix from the data collected during this phase. An example of this matrix is shown in Figure 9-2.

Organization / Process	Product Dev	Manufact'g	Ware./Dist.	Sales	Advertising	Contrlr
Forecast Product	●	X		X		/
Design Product	●	/		/		/
Assemble Product	/	●				
Market Product				●	X	/
Process Order		X	●	X		/
Cntrl Product Inv			●	/		/

For each process, identify the extent of each organization's involvement.

● Primary responsibility
X Major involvement
/ Minor involvement

Figure 9-2   Process vs. Organization Matrix

In order to prioritize any information strategy opportunities, the study team also develops a "process vs. strategy" matrix. An example of this is shown in Figure 9-3.

9.3.7   Define Data Classes

During this phase, data is grouped into related categories called data classes or entities. Future information systems architecture will include databases that contain this data. The organization of these databases should minimize the need for future revisions. Criteria for data categorization are the relationships of the data to the business processes.

The study team will develop three matrices for the defined data classes. They are as follows:

• Matrix usage — Process vs. Data Class

 — Reflects companywide data needs
 — Communicates data sharing by processes

Strategy / Process	Imp Inv Ctl	Strm Ord Cyc	Exp Prod Line	Inc Adv Pen	Central. Inv	Sup Argmnts
Forecast Product	X		X	/	/	
Design Product			X			/
Assemble Product	X		/		X	
Market Product		/		/	/	
Process Order	/	X			X	
Cntrl Product Inv	X	X			X	

For each process, determine impact on each strategy

X Major involvement
/ Minor involvement

Figure 9-3   Process vs. Strategy Matrix

— Aids in defining the application scope of data classes
— Aids in identifying application interdependencies

• Matrix Usage — Strategy vs. Data Class

   — Illustrates the relative importance of data about each entity to the business strategies

• Matrix Usage — Organization vs. Data Class

   — Used to define the focal point of responsibility for data about the entity
   — Used to help interviewees define their data requirements
   — Identifies data-sharing possibilities

Figures 9-4, 9-5, and 9-6 are examples of these matrices.

Process \ Entity	Product	Customer	Cust. Order	Marketplace	Vendor	Part
Forecast Product	●	✕	╱	✕		
Design Product	●		╱	╱	╱	●
Assemble Product	✕					✕
Market Product	✕	●	╱	╱		
Process Order	✕	✕	●			
Cntrl Product Inv	●					

✕ Major usage
╱ Minor usage
● Creates data

Figure 9-4   Entity vs. Process Matrix

Entity / Strategy	Product	Customer	Cust. Order	Marketplace	Vendor	Part
Improve Inv Control	X				/	X
Strmln Order Cycle	/	X	X			
Expand Prod Line	X	/	/	X		/
Inc Adv Penetration		X		X		
Central Inv Mgmt	X				/	X
Supplier Agreements						X

X Major support
/ Minor support

Figure 9-5   Entity vs. Strategy Matrix

Entity / Organization	Product Dev	Manufact'g	Ware./Dist.	Sales	Advertising	Contrlr
Product	●	X	X	X	/	
Customer			X	●		/
Customer Order			X	●		X
Marketplace				X	●	
Vendor	X	●				X
Part	X	●	X	/		/

● Primary Responsibility
X Major usage
/ Minor usage

Figure 9-6   Entity vs. Organization Matrix

9.4   Conducting Executive Interviews

The major purpose of this phase is to validate the understanding that the team has developed thus far. Another purpose is to achieve the commitment and support of executives not yet deeply involved in the study. The executive interviews conducted during this phase provide the study team with a basic understanding of the business problems that the information systems architecture should solve.

A. Preparation for Interviews
    The success of the interviewing process depends to a large extent on the amount of preparation that has gone into conducting the interviews. Preparation for the interviews should include:

   • Verifying interview list with the corporate sponsor
   • Scheduling interviews
   • Developing interviewee briefing
   • Developing a letter to be issued to each interviewee by the corporate sponsor
   • Developing questions tailored to each interviewee
   • Obtaining and preparing interview room
   • Selecting an interview team
   • Assigning roles to each team member
   • Preparing and rehearsing the roles of each team member

B. Conducting the Interviews
    The interview process and the questions asked during the interviews are specifically geared toward obtaining information from the executives about their involvement in the strategies, processes, and data requirements of the organization. During the interviews, the team will do the following:

   • Brief the executives on the objectives, activities, and deliverables of the study
   • Indicate the purpose and flow of the interview
   • Elicit   information   opportunities   by   addressing   the interviewee's need for support for:

     — His business strategy involvement
     — The processes for which he is responsible
     — The data classes that satisfy his business functions
     — His critical success factor

The interviewee should be asked to give a value and priority ranking for each information opportunity. He should also be asked to state his expectations for the future and any additional information opportunities these expectations might entail.

C. The Postinterview Process
   After the interviews are completed, the interview team will:

- Complete the information opportunities details
- Compile notes and create summaries
- Send summaries to interviewee with corrections and/or comments

9.5   Information Opportunity Analysis

The purpose of this phase is to analyze the information opportunities that were discovered during the interviews. It is also during this phase that the study team will develop the necessary support recommendations and prioritize them.

The information opportunities are reviewed for duplication. They are then categorized by process and by data class. This categorization will allow for the identification of applications and the data classes to support each information opportunity. The applications will be prioritized in order to determine a sequence for implementation.

9.6   The Data and Process Architectures

The study team will use the processes and data classes identified earlier in the study to design databases of the future information architecture. The architecture for the processes and data classes will vary from organization to organization. It may consist of a simple list of data entities and their relationships or entity-relationship diagrams at the highest level for the data architecture. A list of the processes and their functions or a data flow diagram may suffice for the process architecture.

The study team will identify major systems and subsystems and determine if some subsystems must be completed before others. The architecture diagrams will reflect the relationship of systems and subsystems.

9.7 Developing Recommendations and Action Plans

The study team will make recommendations not only for systems, subsystems, hardware, and software, but also for adjustments to systems under development to systems currently in production. Another major area of recommendation includes strengthening information systems management with improved planning and control mechanisms identified during the study. The action plan will identify priorities and the means of delivering the future information architecture.

9.8 Format of Final Report

A brief executive summary covers the purpose of the study, its methodology, its conclusions, and its recommendations. A more detailed and comprehensive report expands these topics. In addition, an oral presentation to executives with slides or other visual media should conclude the study.

The report content should be as follows:

• Executive Summary
• Background

— Study Objectives
— Methodology

• Business Perspective

— Business Environment
— Mission, Goals, and Strategies

• Findings

— Enterprise Model
— Information Opportunities/Needs
— Information Management Requirements

• I/S Strategies and Recommendations

— Prioritization Criteria
— I/S Strategies and Recommendations

• Action Plans
• Appendix

9.9 Summary

The Business Systems Plan (BSP) described in this chapter was developed by IBM. The author reported on this plan with very little departure from the BSP course normally given by IBM. The readers are recommended to augment the knowledge gained from this chapter with courses from IBM.

10

Database Architecture
Development

Introduction

This chapter discusses the development of databases and database architecture as they relate to the management of data. It discusses the development of databases for specific applications and business functions. The approach throughout this chapter will be to illustrate how the database effort should have as its primary goal the enhancement of practices that serve to manage data as a corporate resource.

10.1 The Database Environment

Databases and database management systems were developed to overcome the handicap of file-oriented systems. Database technology was intended to serve multiple applications, reducing the need to store data in redundant information systems files. The same data could be accessed by many different applications — and even for new applications yet to be defined.

When companies first began to use DBMSs, they proceeded cautiously, implementing one database-oriented information system at a time. This allowed both the users and members of the management information system (MIS) department to become familiar with the new concepts gradually, without disrupting the whole MIS operation.

However, this seemingly prudent approach resulted in application-oriented database systems, each of which focused on only one particular area of the company. These systems provided some of the benefits of database, but lacked the required flexibility for broad sharing of data in other areas of the company and thus failed to overcome one of the most severe limitations of the original file-oriented systems.

As database technology progressed, the idea of managing data as a company resource, separate from the systems that use the data, became a goal. If data could be organized around company business subjects, instead of being tailored to individual application areas, the resultant structures would be more stable and shareable by everyone.

10.2   A New Approach to Designing Databases

The process of designing information systems for a subject database environment involves more complex factors than did traditional systems design. In addition to systems analysis and design, there are now sophisticated logical and physical data design methods to be considered, as well as data dictionary standards.

A new information system cannot be planned in isolation. It must be conceived and orchestrated with the plans for other information systems and scheduled in concert with a database development plan. In systems development, the organization must evaluate the adequacy of existing data files and make arrangements for their continued maintenance during the lengthy transition to new database systems.

Managing data as a company resource requires coordination of all data and information development tasks relating to both old and new systems.

In a fully developed database environment, the separation between management of company data and management of the systems that use the data must be clear. The organization and management of company data become the responsibility of project development teams, but there is a difference in the way systems data structures are defined.

Each information system development project team performs the detailed systems and data analyses and defines the user views of data that must be made available. In this way, the project team identifies the logical views of company data that are required by a particular information system, without dictating the design of the company-level subject databases.

Within the frameworks of subject databases and their data entities, the data administration organization can then integrate the logical views of data required by this information system project with those of other projects, to create a composite company view of data. The complete company view of data is thus developed over time and results from the collective synthesis of all user views from all information systems projects as they are designed. It is this company logical view of data that is translated into physical database design.

10.3   The Information Systems Architecture

The new approach to designing databases, discussed in the previous section, requires an information systems architecture as the underlying model from which to build databases. This architecture provides the global delineation of all systems required to operate and manage the company by defining information systems which:

- Serve a group of closely related business activities that fall within a single business function
- Communicate only with subject databases, not with other information systems
- Have clearly defined system and project boundaries
- Are manageable as implementation projects and maintainable as operational systems
- Collectively extract data from the subject databases and transform it into the information required by all users to perform business activities
- Collectively capture all of the source data needed to maintain the subject databases in a current state

10.4   Selecting the DBMS

A very important activity in creating the database environment that was discussed earlier is to select a DBMS. The choice of a DBMS is the most critical one that an MIS manager will have to make outside of choosing the mainframe computer. It is therefore very important that this choice be based on as much information as possible. Several organizations have made selection criteria available to prospective buyers. The following list can be added to those.

Database definition facilities: The DBMS should directly and automatically support one-to-many and many-to-many relationships between entities.

Database manipulation facilities: The DBMS should provide data manipulation languages of various types, both procedural and nonprocedural, for end users as well as for information system developers.

Data retrieval facilities: The DBMS should have data retrieval facilities for end users and information system developers.

Access control facilities: The DBMS should provide access control at lead down to the data item level, possibly even down to the value level, to avoid bottlenecks created by file locking.

Backup and recovery facilities: These should be automatic and not solely dependent on the operating system.

Database restructuring facilities: These should give automatic support for database offloading, redefinition, and reloading.

File handling utilities: The trend toward compatibility and equipment integration demands software utilities that harmonize different file formats and database organizations.

Database administrator utilities: These software tools support the need of the database administrator to fine-tune continuously the individual databases.

Data dictionary/directory facilities: Among the most essential data source management tools, these facilities provide intelligence on data resources and support data administration and timely systems development and maintenance.

Application software interface: In many industries there are basic applications that drive the DBMS selection process. Therefore, the system that best supports the selected application software has a major competitive advantage.

Datacom software interface: For organizations that are widely dispersed geographically, the DBMS that best supports its datacom software configuration has a competitive advantage.

Machine efficiency: Companies with large volumes of transactions to be processed soon learn that not all DBMSs are alike when it comes to machine efficiency. Several firms report that they incurred substantial conversion costs replacing a DBMS that failed in a high-transaction volume environment.

Degree of data independence: The ability of the DBMS to divorce the logical database definition from the way it's physically stored increases opportunities for changing both things. Similar benefits are derived from a DBMS that separates the logical database definition from the many user views — queries or application programs.

Compatibility with other DBMSs: To satisfy today's wide variety of MIS needs, most organizations are likely to acquire more than one DBMS. To share the company's data resources, it is necessary for these different systems to be able to freely transfer data back and forth.

Training time/costs: As the number of a DBMS's users grow, the necessary training time and costs increase correspondingly. Companies are interested in two phases: the training time needed for elementary, productive work, and the time it takes to achieve proficiency with a particular package.

Ease of use: Once the user has learned how to work with DBMS, the flexibility of the language, the transparency of the functions, and the system's ability to support applications become critical considerations.

Vendor support: A key selection criterion is the ability and willingness of the DBMS vendor to resolve customer problems in such areas as implementation and machine performance. The vendor's knowledge about the DBMS internals is essential for a prompt and effective solution to these problems.

User group strength: The existence and strength of a large group of organizations using the specific DBMS is an important selection factor. It increases the likelihood that the product will be maintained and improved by the vendor as well as by third parties.

10.5 Data Structures for Databases

One of the major responsibilities of the data administration function is the development of an enterprise or data model of the organization. The model embodies the entities and their relationships and is the tool used to represent the conceptual organization of data. The model is a tool for communication between the various users, so it is developed without any concern for physical representation. It is used to organize, visualize, plan, and communicate ideas. It is independent of a DBMS.

The entities of an organization and the relationships between them can be represented by a data model. The DBMSs available commercially today are based on a hierarchical data model, a network data model, or a relational data model.

The enterprise model has to be mapped to the logical model being used as the underlying structure for a DBMS, and the logical model must be mapped to the physical model. The logical model is a relational, a hierarchical, or a network data model.

10.5.1 The Hierarchical Data Model

A hierarchical tree structure is made up of nodes and branches. A node is a collection of data attributes describing the entity at that node. The highest node of a hierarchical tree structure is called a "root." The dependent notes are at lower levels in the tree.

A hierarchical data model is one that organizes data in a hierarchical tree structure. Every occurrence of the root node begins a logical database record.

A hierarchical tree structure has to satisfy the following conditions:

- A hierarchical data model always starts with a "root" node
- Every node consists of one or more attributes describing the entity at that node
- Dependent nodes can follow the succeeding levels. The node on the preceding level becomes the "parent node" of the new "dependent nodes." The dependent nodes can be added horizontally as well as vertically with no limitation.
- Every node occurring at level 2 has to be connected with one and only one node occurring at level 1.

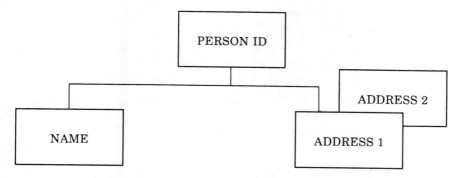

Figure 10-1   Hierarchical Data Model

In Figure 10-1, the "parent" node is PERSON, and the "child" nodes are NAME and ADDRESS. It should be noted that the dependent nodes have one and only one node occurring at the higher level.

10.5.2   The Relational Data Model

The data in a relational data model is represented in a two-dimensional table, called a relational model of the data. In the relational data model terminology, a table is called a relation. Every column in a relation is an attribute. The values in the column are drawn from a domain or set of all the values an attribute may have. The rows of the table are called Tuples.

In Figure 10-2, a column or set of columns is called a candidate key (or key) when its values uniquely identify the rows of the table. It is also possible for a relation to have more than one key, in which case it is customary to designate one as the primary key.

10.5.3   The Network Data Model

The network data model interconnects the entities of an enterprise into a network. The basic difference between the hierarchical data model and network is that the network data model allows a dependent node to have more than one owner, whereas the hierarchical model allows only one owner.

The network data model establishes unique ownership by group member and owner records into a set. Thus, at any one time a member record can belong to only one set type.

PERSON TABLE		
PERSON ID	**NAME**	**ADDRESS**
1111	John White	15 New St., N.Y.
1234	Mary Jones	10 Main St., Rye, N.Y.
2345	Charles Brown	Dogwood Lane, Harrison, N.Y.

Figure 10-2   Relational Data Model

In Figure 10-3, the dependent node ENGINE is "owned" simultaneously by the nodes CAR and TRUCK. At any one time, the CAR-ENGINE relationship forms one set type, and at another time, the TRUCK-ENGINE relationship forms another set type.

10.5.4   Advantages and Disadvantages of These Models

The information resource manager, when selecting a DBMS for his organization, must weigh the advantages and disadvantages of each of the three major data models discussed earlier. As in selecting the DBMS, the resource manager must outline a set of criteria for advantages and disadvantages of each DBMS.

The author does not intend to list the advantages and disadvantages of each major DBMS here. I will leave that for each resource manager as a research task.

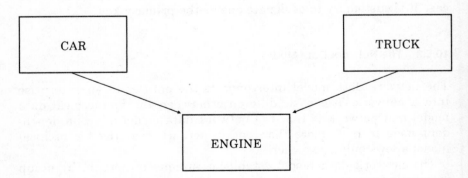

Figure 10-3   Network Data Model

10.6   Development of Specific Database Architectures

Very often because of the complexity of the data management task an organization may be forced to develop complex database architecture for specific applications. The author was involved in such a task several years ago. The account of such an undertaking is reported in the rest of this chapter. The database architecture reported on was developed for an advanced office information system. It allowed a user to make inquiries as to a specific product available from an advanced office information system. This user's identification is authenticated when he makes an inquiry by telephone, an interactive terminal, or directly to the central processing unit (CPU) via a batch job.

When it has been verified that the user is authorized to make an inquiry, the database design allows for the determination of the validity of the request made by the user.

The architecture supports a series of users' requests identified as to which details the types of services the user is authorized to request and receive.

After the user's request is verified, the type and availability of the output media is then verified. Certain users and products are cross-referenced by the architecture. This eliminates the possibility of a user gaining access to an output medium to which he is not entitled.

Once the product request is verified, the architecture then determines the state of readiness for delivery of the product. If the product can be readily available, the component responsible for delivery prepares the product for delivery to the user. If the product is not available, outdated, or must be altered in some fashion, this fact is recorded by Event Monitoring and tagged for future delivery.

Event Monitoring constantly polls its query for the time of delivery of a product. When the time to deliver a product has arrived, that fact is conveyed to Product Fabrication and Delivery for delivery to the user.

The architecture also allows for the creation of audit trails, which allow the responsible people to monitor events as they occur in each component of the architecture.

10.6.1   Overview of Components of Architecture

Figure 10-4 is a diagram of the basic components of the architecture and the interfaces between each component.

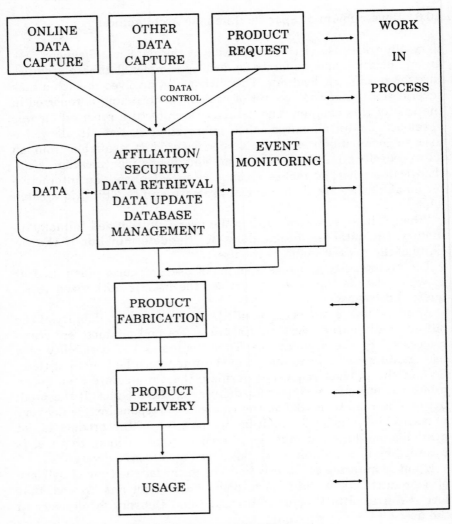

Figure 10-4 Components of Database Architecture

Communication between the components is maintained through calling or called parameters. For example, the Data Capture component will pass the user identification and password to Data Control for authentication and verification. Data Control will verify the identification and return the status to Data Capture.

10.6.2   Interfaces Between Components

The interfaces between components are of two types:

1) Standard Interface
2) Specific Interface

10.6.3   Standard Interface Elements

The Standard Interface consists of the following elements:

a) Session Identifier/Reference Number — Identifies the application system, the input media, the date and time of the initial system recognition.
b) Subject Identifier — Identifies the entity on which the initial session operates.
c) Process Date — Current business process date.
d) Process Time — Current time.
e) Request Type — Identifies the entity (report) type and action to be performed.
f) Entity Identifier — One or more keys used to identify the report or reports to be acted on.

10.6.4   Specific Interface Elements

The Specific Interface consists of the following elements:

a) Access Area — Identifies whether the retrieval/update is from/to a work area or the database.
b) Element Value — Specifies the values used/to applied in performing an action.
c) New Status — Specifies a new logical event, status or result of a component interface to be stored in the work in process entry.
d) Search Ceiling — The maximum number of match candidates to be returned.
e) Search Threshold — The minimum rank or score required in order to be considered a match candidate.
f) Product Identifier — Name or symbol that identifies a product.
g) Product Content — Makeup of product.

h) Delivery Media — The media to which the product is to be delivered.

i) Suitability Override — Identifies the option to override suitability checking.

Figures 10-5 and 10-6 illustrate the component/subcomponent interfaces with another component. For example, Data Update invokes Data Retrieval, Data Element Deviation, Work on Process Track, and Event Monitoring.

10.6.5   Examples of Interfacing in the Architecture

The following interfacing patterns are found in the database architecture:

a) Data Capture invokes Work on Process to obtain the Session Identifier.

b) Data Control is invoked to validate the Userid, Password, and to obtain the Session Profile.

c) Data Capture invokes Entity Identification Search to obtain Trade Experience match candidates. Entity Identification Search invokes Data Retrieval to obtain the necessary data. Data Capture invokes work on process to record choice. Data Retrieval is invoked by Data Capture.

10.6.6   Processing Details of Each Component

The following sections describe the processing details of each component.

A. Data Capture Component
   The Data Capture component carries out the following functions:

- Online and bulk capture of data from external sources.
- Updates single or multiple entities.
- Insulate capture of external data from knowledge of database structure and update logic.
- Present Standard Interface to Data Control.

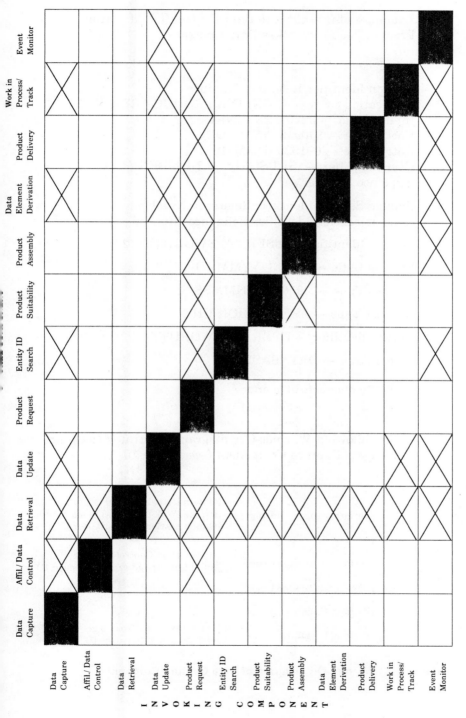

Figure 10-5 Database Architecture Interfaces

1. Examples of interfaces to Data Control (for Affiliation)
2. Product Request invokes Data Control

Interface

Session Identifier/Reference Number
Application System — ONLINE PRODUCT REQUEST
Input Media — 3270 TERMINAL
Entry Date — 840913 (YYMMDD)
Entry Time — 091620 (HHMMSS)
User Identifier — (SUBSCRIBER NUMBER)
Sequence Number — 01

Related Session Identifier/Reference Number
same as Session Identifier/Reference Number

Subject Identifier — USER PASSWORD [YY123]

Process Date — 840913 (YYMMDD)

Process Time — 091621 (HHMMSS)

Request Type — AFFILIATION CHECK

Entity Identifier — USER PASSWORD [YY123]

Access Area — DATABASE

Figure 10-6   Components of Interface

The following Warnier-Orr diagram illustrates the functions of the Data Capture Component (see Figure 10-7).

	Performs Logon/Startup	Obtain logon information Invoke Work in Process to start Audit Obtain session ID, mark user ID in use
DataCapture	Perform Affiliation Check	Invoke Data Control to check affiliation ID and retrieve session ID
	Obtain Entities for Update	
	Perform Updates	
	Perform Logoff/End of Job	Invoke Work in Process to end Audit and free user ID

Figure 10-7   Warnier-Orr Diagram of Data Capture Component

B. Data Control Component

The Data Control component carries out the following functions:

- Performs logical and physical management of all data.
- Insulates other components from knowledge of logical and physical management of data.
- Unifies all subfunctions; e.g., Data Retrieval or Affiliation/Security into a unified process.
- Retrieves data from all databases.
- Insulates other components from knowledge of retrieval logic and logical database structure.
- Determines whether user exists and is valid.
- Determines whether user is authorized for requested retrieval or update.
- Updates all databases.
- Performs physical to logical mapping.
- Performs logical to physical mapping.
- Generates actual DBMS calls.
- Insulates other components from knowledge of physical database structure and DBMS implementation.

The following Warnier-Orr diagram illustrates the functions of Data Control (see Figure 10-8).

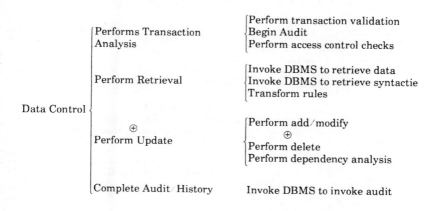

Note: ⊕ *is an exclusive OR.*

Figure 10-8   Warnier-Orr Diagram of Data Control Componenet

C. Product Management Component

The Product Management component carries out the following functions:

- Performs all processing required to assemble and deliver products.
- Accepts online or bulk requests.
- Accommodates dynamic and static products.
- Accommodates single and multiple entity products.
- Accommodates search parameters and user-supplied product definition.

The following Warnier-Orr diagram illustrates the functions of Product Request Subcomponent of the Product Management Component (see Figure 10-9).

Product Request
{

Perform Logon / Startup Analysis
{ Obtain logon information
Invoke Work in Process to start audit

Perform Affiliation check
{ Invoke Data Control to check affiliation ID, retrieve session profile

Obtain products awaiting delivery
⊕
Obtain entities for fabrication

Process Product Request
{ Select product
Obtain product content
Perform delivery processing

Logoff
{ Invoke Work in Process to end audit and free user ID

Note: ⊕ *is an exclusive* OR.

Figure 10-9   Warnier-Orr Diagram of Product Request Subcomponent

D. Event Monitoring Component

The Event Monitoring component carries out the following functions:

- Triggers processes sensitive to changes in data element values.
- Triggers processes sensitive to time changes.
- Insulates other components from knowledge of logic controlling these processes.

The following Warnier-Orr diagram illustrates the functions of the Event Monitoring component of the database architecture (see Figure 10-10).

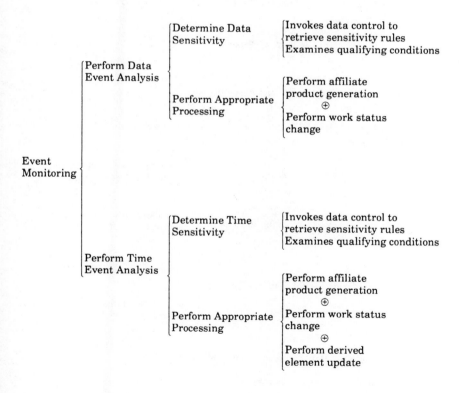

Note: ⊕ is an exclusive OR.

Figure 10-10   Warnier-Orr Diagram of Event Monitoring Component

E. Work in Process Component

The Work in Process component carries out the following functions:

• Maintains an active audit trail of all the database inquiries and updates.
• Provides a trigger mechanism for recording of product/service usage.
• Allows for individual transaction audit, work profile over time, and capability to ensure completion of processing.
• Provides mechanism for archiving of statistics.

The following Warnier-Orr diagram illustrates one of the functions of the Work in Process component of the database architecture (see Figure 10-11).

Perform Affiliate Product Generation {

Invoke Work in Process to start audit

Invoke Product Assembly

Immediate delivery   Invoke Product Delivery
        ⊕

Deferred delivery   { Invoke Work in Process to record (deferred) status
        ⊕

Unsuitable for fabrication   { Invoke Work in Process to record (unsuitable) status

Note: ⊕ is an exclusive OR.

Add New Audit Trail {

Generate logical session identifier

Form new audit trail   { Logical session identifier application specific data new status

Test Context

Activate Data Control to store new trail

Increment status counts

Return results   Logical session identifier status

Figure 10-11   Warnier-Orr Diagram of Work in Process Component

10.6.7   Rules and Assertions for the Database Architecture

Data processing in the database architecture is accomplished by a
series of rules and assertions.
  These include:

• Access Rules
• Schema Generation
• Data Relationship
• Allowable View
• Completeness Test
• Security
• Syntax
• Accounting and Job Management
• Mapping of Physical/Logical Views
• Specialized Delivery Rules

10.6.8   List of Database Architecture Tables

The database architecture was supported by the following tables:

• Userid and Passwords
• Entity Security
• Product Profile
• Subschema and Schema
• DBMS Address Table
• Subscribe Codes
• Valid Path
• Tolerance Table

10.6.9   Narrative of Tables

The following sections describe the tables and rules used by the
database architecture.

  A. Userid and Password
      The Userid and Password tables are unique identifiers re-
  quired by the log-on process of the architecture. These identifiers are authenticated by the Affiliation/Security subcomponent
  of Data Control and are key components of the user profiles.

B. Entity Security

The Entity Security table forms part of the user profile table used by Affiliation/Security to determine the access authorization of a user and the products he/she is entitled to during a particular session.

C. Product Profile Table

The Product Profile table is a list of products and combination of products available to the subscriber and supported by the architecture.

D. Schema and Subschema

The Schema and Subschema table includes the list of application programming, data views, and data relationships necessary for data retrieval and update are all contained in the schema table. A particular user requirement for data will constitute a subschema table.

E. Valid Path Table

The Valid Path table is used by Work in Process to create audit trails. It defines navigation paths a transaction would take to arrive at the required data.

10.6.10   Narrative of Control Data Rules

The following sections describe the rules of the database architecture.

A. Derivation Rules

Rules designed to produce data elements for immediate display or storage in the DBIS database, for example, trade input handlers.

B. Validation and Update Rules

Rules that specify the conditions that must be satisfied before an element in the database can be updated. The validation rules will be used to check for consistency and integrity in data elements; verify and authenticate users of the system; verify product content and association, produce delivery formats and media; and in general, indicate what are allowable conditions, processes, and entities in the DBIS environment.

C. Access Rules

Determine the authority needed, the conditions that must be met, and what can be done once inside the system by a user desiring access to the DBIS environment. They will state the mode, whether direct or indirect, available to the user to access data.

D. Schemas and Schema Content Rules

Rules used to determine and create the logical data structures and relationships among data elements. The rules would indicate what the content of each schema should be and the local or user views that can be made from the schemas. These rules would not indicate any logical/physical mapping of data.

E. Subschemas and User View Rules

These rules will indicate the minimum content of a user view, the user/view relationship, the requirements to create dynamic or user requested views, and any cross-reference to schemas requirements.

F. Allowable User View Rules

Because of product content, user/product relationship, data element security, or delivery medium/product relationship, some user views may not be permissible.

G. Cross-Sectional Validation Rules

These rules describe the interrelationship among data elements in a single view or several views and indicate what relationships are permissible.

H. Completeness Test Rules

The Completeness Test rules are rules to indicate what steps should be taken to determine that the auditing of a transaction is complete; processing against the database is complete, for example, in order for an update to be complete a status code must be returned to the requesting component; consistency/integrity checks are complete; and the schemas and views are complete and adequate.

I. Security and Granularity of Security Rules

These rules define the measure of security that will be accorded such items as views, schemas, and data elements. They will also describe the protection mechanism used; e.g., password, user profile, or RACF. The granularity rules will define the level of protection given to each item.

The rules can also include consistency/integrity rules.

10.7   Summary

This chapter discussed the development of database architecture to aid in the management of data as a resource. The chapter omitted the theory of databases since this can easily be obtained in the available literature. It ended with a detailed discussion of an architecture developed to allow users to access an advanced office information system.

11

Case Tools in Systems Design

Introduction

Computer-aided software engineering (CASE) has been promoted as
the panacea for curing an organization's backlog problems in meeting
development schedules, coordinating design efforts, and maintaining
its systems. It has also been touted as the tool to increase programmer and systems designer productivity as much as 2- to 10-fold.

This chapter will introduce CASE tools as a design and development aid. It will discuss some selection criteria for deciding on the
tool that will best suit a particular environment. Finally, it will list
some vendors of CASE tools and the contracts within each vendor.

11.1 Several Introductory Remarks

CASE, although now widely accepted as an acronym, does not yet
have a single, widely accepted definition. Perhaps a more appropriate acronym would be CASD (computer-aided systems development),
which could be defined as "computers applied to aid in any aspect of
systems development."

Because CASE can encompass so many aspects of systems development, the question "When is CASE the right choice?" must be addressed separately for each of three types of CASE tools:

1. Programmer/Project Productivity Tools — Provide support for designers and programmers of software, but only at the back end of the systems development life cycle. These may include tools for natural language programming, project management, and documentation.
2. Systems Development Methodology Tools — Most systems development methodologies are collections of techniques, combined in structures made to minimize redundant effort and maximize coordination between tasks. These methodology tools provide support for and enforce a systems development methodology at any or all stages of the life cycle. They may include any of the systems development support tools as appropriate for the methodology. In addition, they enforce methodology rules and thus provide systems development expertise to the users.
3. Systems Development Support Tools — Provide support for techniques and tasks of systems development at any or all stages of the life cycle, but do not necessarily enforce a systems development methodology. These may include diagramming tools, data dictionaries and analysis tools, or any of the productivity tools.

11.2 Categories of CASE Tools

An individual CASE tool automates one small, focused step in the life-cycle process. Individual tools fall into these general categories:

- Diagramming tools for pictorially representing system specifications.
- Screen and report painters for creating system specifications for simple prototyping.
- Dictionaries, information management systems, and facilities to store, report and query technical and project-management system information.
- Specification-checking tools to detect incomplete, syntactically incorrect, and inconsistent system specifications.
- Code generators to be able to generate executable code from pictorial system specifications.
- Documentation generators to product technical and user documentation required by structured methodologies.

CASE "toolkits" provide integrated tools for developers seeking to automate only one phase of the life cycle process, while "workbenches" provide integrated tools for automating the entire development process. "Frameworks" integrate CASE tools and/or link them with non-CASE software development tools, and "methodology companions" support a particular structured methodology and automatically guide developers through the development steps.

11.2.1 Well-Equipped Toolkits

Toolkits can focus on the design of real-time, information, or project management systems. They also can be classified by the hardware and operating system on which they run; by the ease with which they can be integrated into a family of compatible CASE tools; by their architecture (open, so that it can be used with products from other vendors, or closed, by the structured methodology or methodologies they support); and by development languages such as Ada, Cobol, Fortran, C, and PL/1.

Many CASE toolkits run on an IBM PC or compatible under DOS. Some run on the Apple Macintosh, Wang PC, or Texas Instruments Professional PC. Others run only on 32-bit workstations, such as Sun, Apollo, or Digital Equipment Corporation (DEC) Vax Station II, on an IBM or Data General mainframe, or across the DEC Vax family. Many open-architecture products are not limited to one specific hardware, operating system, target programming language, or structured methodology.

The analysis toolkit has four basic components: structured diagramming tools, prototyping tools, a repository, and a specification checker.

11.2.2 Structured Diagramming Tools

Structured diagramming tools are computerized tools for drawing, manipulating, and storing structured diagrams such as data-flow and entity-relationship diagrams, which are required documentation for various structured methodologies.

Diagramming tools often reside on PCs or workstations that support graphics manipulation; at the minimum, they draw, update, and store data-flow and entity-relationship diagrams.

11.2.3   Prototyping Tools

Prototyping tools help determine system requirements and predict performance beforehand. Essential to prototyping are user-interface painters — screen painters, report painters, and menu builders — that prototype the user interface to give users an advance view of how the system will look and to identify and correct problem areas. Screen dialog and navigation with data entry and edits can be simulated with or without compiles; source code for record, file, screen, and report description can be generated automatically.

Also essential are executable specification languages. These are the most sophisticated prototyping tools, which involve specifying system requirements and executing specifications iteratively to refine, correct, and ensure completeness of the system to meet user requirements.

11.2.4   The CASE Repository

The CASE repository is a design dictionary for storing and organizing all software system data, diagrams, and documentation related to planning, analysis, design, implementation, and project management. Information entered once can be maintained and made available to whomever needs it.

The repository stored more types of systems information, relationships among various information components, and rules for using or processing components than a standard data dictionary used in data management systems. The repository usually has many reporting capabilities that gauge the impact of proposed changes on the system, identify redundant or unneeded data elements, and resolve discrepancies. System diagrams and dictionary entities are linked within the dictionary, and some CASE tools provide automated means of verifying entities for completeness and correctness.

11.2.5   Data Design Toolkits

These tools support the logical and physical design of databases and files: logical data modeling, automatic conversion of data models to third-normal form, automatic generation of database schemes for particular database management systems, and automatic generation of program-code level file descriptions.

11.2.6   Programming Toolkits

Supported tools include hierarchical tree-structured diagramming tools with a syntax and consistency checker; procedural logic diagrammer and online editor; CASE repository with information manager; code generation; test data generator; file comparer; and performance monitor.

A code-generating tool is especially useful because it automatically produces codes from a program design. CASE code generators can generate compiled, structured codes in languages such as Cobol, PL/1, Fortran, C, or Ada, manage program specification and design information, generate documentation, and support prototyping.

11.2.7   Maintenance Toolkits

The most useful maintenance tools include documentation analyzers to read source code from existing systems and produce documentation, program analyzers, to evaluate execution paths and performance; reverse engineering to identify the model upon which a system is based; and restructures to enforce structured programming and documentation standards.

11.2.8   Project Management Toolkits

Automated project management tools can help project managers better track, control, and report on software projects, thus improving software development and maintenance. To be most effective, these tools should be able to access the CASE repository in the toolkit or workbench. Besides storing technical system information, the repository should be the central location for current status, estimation, budget and quality-assurance information.

Some of these toolkits include tools for work processing; interfacing to electronic mail; spreadsheets; project-management forms; configuration management for change, version, and access control; project plans; a calendar and task assignment system; and estimation of time tables and scheduling.

11.3   Demonstrated Use of CASE Tools in the SDLC

CASE tools have demonstrated their usefulness in all three components of the CASE environment: planning, systems design, and systems development.

11.3.1   CASE in the Planning Environment

CASE tools gather information about user problems and requirements; setting goals and criteria; generating alternative solutions.

They assist in the budget determinations; project duration and scheduling; manpower planning and scheduling; cost and time estimates; and project control.

11.3.2   CASE in the Systems Design Environment

CASE tools detail the design for a selected solution, including diagrams relating all programs, subroutines, and data flow.

They can generate data modeling and relationship diagrams and functional models.

The functional modeling and data modeling processes have tools to construct the appropriate types of design diagrams. Data-flow diagrams, program structure charts, and entity-relationship diagrams are examples of diagrams.

More detailed tables and text contain the necessary concept descriptions, testable requirements, and data element definitions.

11.3.3   CASE in the Systems Development Environment

CASE tools develop a construct of database information about the physical database scheme and the requirements for building, testing, and checking databases. They produce language codes from definitions of data and processes stored in the data dictionary.

11.3.4 Samples of Deliverables from CASE Tools

The next several pages illustrate the deliverables from the three components of the CASE environment.

The deliverables in Figures 11-1 through 11-4 were produced from the following sample problem:

Our sample problem concerns a video rental store with the following:

• Customer rents tapes and makes rental payments
• Customer returns tapes and may pay late charge of $1 per day

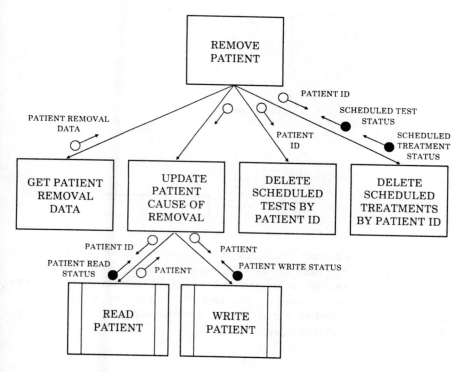

Figure 11-1 Yourdon Structure Chart. *A structure chart is a tree or hierarchical diagram that shows the overall design of the program, including program modules and their relationships. This particular structure chart was produced by the Analyst/Designer Toolkit from Yourdon Inc.*

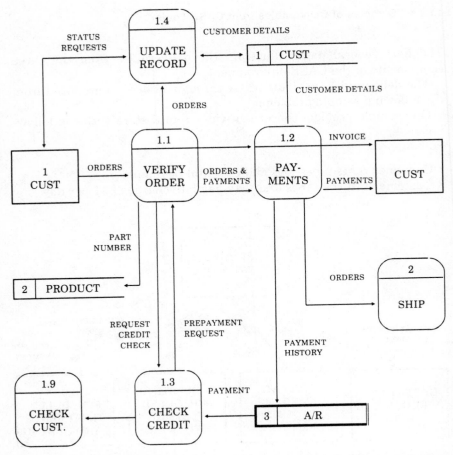

Figure 11-2 Excelerator Produced Data-Flow Diagram. *A data-flow diagram traces the flow of data through a system. Data stores are indicated by open-end rectangles, processes by boxes with rounded corners, data flow by arrows, and external entities by squares. This diagram was produced by Excelerator from Index Technology Corp., using the Gene and Sarson technique.*

- Time to notify overdue borrowers
- Time to report rentals
- Store submits new tape

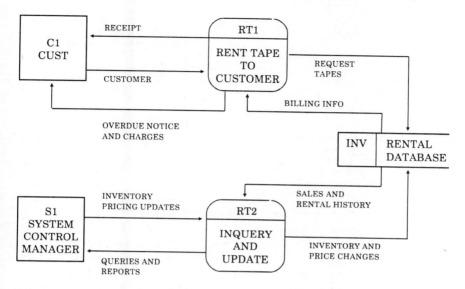

Figure 11-3   Excelerator Produced Data-Flow Diagram.

- Store submits rate changes in some movie titles
- Customer changes address
- Customer requests particular movie title

The standard time period for a rental is two days after the borrowed tape is rented. If the customer fails to return the tape in time, then it is time to send a tape overdue notice to the customer address with the title and copy number and past due return date.

A tape is a videotape cassette with a prerecorded movie that can be rented. Each tape has a movie title and copy number. All copies of a movie have the same rental rate. Not all movies have the same rental rate.

A rental is the lending of a tape to a person in exchange for cash. A rental has a check-out date, a return date, and a rental charge. If a tape is late, there is a standard $1 per day late charge paid upon return. A customer can rent more than one tape at a time.

A tape can be rented, on the shelf waiting to be rented, or overdue. This video store has no membership plan and doesn't take American Express. All transactions are in cash, and no deposits are accepted.

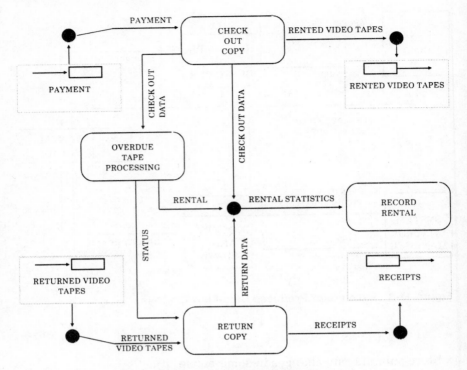

Figure 11-4   Knowledgeable Produced Data-Flow Diagram

11.4   Selection Criteria for CASE Tools

The ever-growing array of CASE tools makes it very difficult to decide which tool is best suited for a particular environment. This section attempts to ease that uncertainty by setting down a list of questions the buyer should seek answers to before buying a tool.

The questions are as follows:

- Is the tool a DBMS or dictionary software system? Dictionary and
  database management systems provide greater integration capabilities. As a result, CASE tools with these underlying structures
  have a greater capacity for sharing specifications across functions.
- What is the future direction and functionality of the tool? When
  evaluating CASE tools, remember that CASE systems development
  is still in its infancy, so don't reject a tool with valuable attributes
  just because it currently does not have the full capabilities that
  you want.

- Does the tool's manufacturer have an open architecture philosophy? A manufacturer's willingness to share file formats with all viable, noncompeting CASE manufacturers means that you can move smoothly from planning through to systems development because you will be able to integrate specifications across CASE components. Moreover, you will have a healthy variety of options for CASE software configurations. CASE manufacturers entering into exclusive hierarchical integration agreements with other noncompeting CASE tool manufacturers ultimately limits choice.
- Does the CASE tool produce utility software that will read procedure and source libraries and create CASE component specifications for existing systems? The acquisition of CASE tools in a non-CASE environment creates a potential for inconsistencies in maintenance activities. Design and development specifications for systems designed and implemented before the installation of CASE components will not be consistent with those created after installation of CASE tools. Thus, a multiplicity of maintenance activities will be necessary. Certain CASE tools offer utility software that will ready procedure and source libraries and create development specifications for existing systems, thereby mitigating the difference between pre-CASE and post-CASE systems documentation.
- Does the tool have an effective interface to other CASE design tools already purchased or under evaluation? Often, several methodologies are used to design a system, so it is important that a CASE tool provide a healthy array of methodological techniques to use in the process. The dictionary entries must be capable of being shared across these methodologies, so the dictionary should be strong and versatile.
- Does the tool have graphical methodologies capable of "exploding" design diagrams and dictionary specifications to a reasonable depth? Most of the CASE design tools provide graphical methodologies for representing proposed systems design. The graphical diagrams and the dictionary entries behind the components of the graphical diagrams must be capable of exploding to a reasonable number of lower, more specific levels.
- Will the tool be capable of executing with windowing capabilities? An advantage of the windowing capability is that multiple portions of the design can be displayed simultaneously and can therefore compensate for weaknesses in embedded explosion capabilities. As a result, the levels of explosion will not be restrictive and the comprehensiveness and integration of CASE design and development specifications should improve.

- Does the planning model in the CASE planning component provide comprehensive coverage of corporate and functional unit strategic planning and systems planning? The planning component contains a model for representing the corporation and for use in determining the direction of the corporation and systems development. The strength of the CASE top-level components lies in the comprehensiveness of this planning model.
- Does the tool provide a thorough means of prototyping? CASE development tools, rather than CASE design tools, provide the strongest prototyping methods. While it is not necessary that both types provide strong prototyping capabilities, at least one must provide this capability.
- Will the tool soon be able to generate automatically first-cut physical design specifications from logical design specifications? The conversion of logical design diagrams into initial physical design diagrams should be automatic because it involves simply the exchange and addition of graphical display table entries. While most CASE design tools currently do not offer this feature, ask your CASE vendor if the tool will offer it in the future.
- Does the CASE design tool provide analysis support for design documentation? This concerns the capacity of the CASE tool to analyze design documentation and determine if the specifications entered by the analyst conform to prescribed methodological rules. The analysis should also indicate where design dictionary entries are incomplete. For example, a DFD diagram with a freestanding block should be highlighted as violating one of the rules of structured methodology. In addition, blocks on a DFD not having corresponding dictionary entry should be highlighted.
- Does the tool have the capacity to generate design specification reports automatically? The specifications created during logical and physical design activities serve as a source of documentation for the system. While they are permanently stored on disk devices, it is often advisable to get hard copy printouts of the design specifications for reference. Many CASE tools provide various report formats for this purpose, including the capability of indicating design flaws.
- Does the lower-level CASE development component provide methods for convenience and comprehensive customization of the generated system? The CASE development component can already generate the major portions of the codes systems. Systems development activity using CASE involves providing the customization of the generic code to fit the system. The custom specifications must provide comprehensive coverage of the system requirements. The

generated programs must also be able to call on existing routines to prevent the system from "reinventing the wheel."

- Does the tool permit distribution of design/development responsibilities? CASE design and development tools must provide a serviceable means of segregating job responsibilities and interfacing the individual efforts into a single system project.

- Does the CASE design and development tool have the capacity to export portions of the design and development dictionary specifications? This is important, as design and development specifications for one system may be reusable in the design and development of other systems. "Reusable design" will join "reusable code" as a result of this capability.

- Can the tool interface design and development specifications to the functional DBMS be used to maintain the company's data? It is rare to develop systems that are not affected by the database environment, and the development of systems using CASE tools is no exception. Therefore, it is important that the CASE tools can interface design and development specifications of application systems to mainframe DBMSs and database creation or modification.

- Does the tool have word processing capabilities? In addition to built-in word processing capabilities, the tool should have an effective interface with standard word processing systems. An added feature of some tools is the ability to pass documentation to a desktop publishing software system for more professional representation.

- Does the tool enhance project management? The use of CASE tools does not preclude the need for effective project management. In fact, their use can enhance such management. Specifications that are entered using a planning component provide a boundary for design and development activities. This boundary provides a built-in means of determining when design and development activities diverge from originally planned specifications. Some CASE design and development tools can generate reports on the progress of individual project assignments, and some can interface to existing project management software systems. Currently, this interface is a temporary exit from the CASE tool into the project management system, but the interface will become much stronger in the future and provide more automatic updating of the project schedule.

- Is it possible to modify the CASE design and development tools relative to your firm's internal or existing methodology? CASE tools are prepackaged systems and may need modifications to make them more suitable for individual installations. Thus, it is important that the system has the ability to add or delete menu options or to modify the style of graphical or dictionary entry screens.

- Can the tool automatically generate design, operations, and end-user documentation? As systems are designed and developed with CASE tools, documentation concerning components and users of the system are entered into the dictionary. Thus, the majority of design, operations, and user documentation required for documentation manuals is available from these dictionary entries. CASE systems should provide this documentation in either online or hard copy form, with little additional work required from the project development team.

- Does the tool have facilities for maintaining design as well as systems? When conditions in business warrant changes in the information systems function, the people responsible for maintenance should be able to effect the required system changes in the system's design specifications automatically. Or once those changes are made, the development tool should be able to designate where the current systems need changing, as well as indicate which users need to be notified of the changes and what they need to be told. Some development systems already provide some of these capabilities. As the interface between CASE design and development software systems becomes stronger, modifications to design specifications entered into the design software will be able to modify development specifications, and, ultimately, the entire system. Since the planning component was the last to emerge, the interface between it and the design component is weak. Subsequently, as the interface between it and the design strengthens, it should have the same effect on those activities as the strengthening of the interface between design and development did.

- Can the tool generate programs that span a range of systems? The hardware and software to create a transparent micro, mini, and mainframe environment are not far off. Consequently, the programs that the CASE tool generates must be able to provide the same execution services on a desktop micro as on a mighty mainframe. Some of today's CASE development systems already offer this.

It goes without saying that the CASE tool manufacturer should be willing to provide a list of installations using its software and grant permission to contact them. This major criterion should govern the purchase of any software system. Should a software vendor refuse to supply this information, you have reason to doubt the validity and comprehensiveness of its product.

11.4.1   Analysis of Selection Criteria

A subset of the above questions was sent to about a dozen vendors of CASE tools. The responses are discussed in another book on CASE tools by the author — *Systems Design in a Database Environment*.

11.5   Vendors of CASE Tools

This section lists some of the major vendors of CASE tools and gives a brief summary of their products.

11.5.1   Vendor List

ADPAC COMPUTING LANGUAGES CORP. Adpac Computing Languages Corporation develops, markets, and services technology support tools for the IBM mainframe operating under MVS. Adpac's CASE tools (DPDP and DESIGN) provide a front-end CAD/CAM diagramming technique that assists analysts in drawing any type of diagram and design analysis with the capability to verify the contents of diagrams.

AGS MANAGEMENT SYSTEMS, INC. AGS/MS is recognized as the world's leader in systems development methodologies and project management system. MULTI/CAM, the micro-mainframe CASE system created by AGS/MS, integrates software development tools, software design and production models, project management, and any other user-selected CASE tools into a unified, automated work environment.

AMERICAN MANAGEMENT SYSTEMS AMS is a major computer services firm specializing in applications development. AMS's Life-cycle Productivity System (LPS) integrates productivity tools from AMS and other vendors for strategic system planning, design, development, maintenance, and project management. LPS produces all deliverable work products required by most methodologies. Major portions of LPS operate on PCs. Implementation, configuration control, and foundation software modules operate on IBM mainframe.

ANALYSTS INTERNATIONAL CORP. Analysts International Corporation, a professional data processing software and services company and a leader in the computer industry for over 22 years, introduces

CORVET. CORVET is a graphics-oriented, PC-based, interactive CASE design and development product that generates stand-alone Cobol programs and comprehensive documentation for IBM mainframe environments.

ARTHUR ANDERSEN & CO. FOUNDATION is a computer-integrated environment for software engineering developed by our consulting practice. Covering the entire systems development life cycle, FOUNDATION consists of METHOD/1, a PC LAN-based tool for planning and design, and INSTALL/1, an IBM mainframe-based environment for implementation and support of DB2 applications.

ARTHUR YOUNG & CO. Arthur Young is an international accounting, tax, and management consulting firm which is working with KnowledgeWare to develop the Information Engineering Workbench (AY/IEW), and markets KnowledgeWare products internationally and uses the AY/IEW for systems building. Arthur Young will present its experience building systems using the AY/IEW and Information Engineering techniques.

ASYST TECHNOLOGIES, INC. The DEVELOPER provides multiuser, automated support for the systems development process, through its repository located either at the PC, at the mainframe (using DB2) or at both sites. The DEVELOPER and its CUSTOMIZER module allow the use of any methodology at all levels of compliance and rigor. Repository integrity is maintained through a menu-driven SQL query language and built-in ASYSTants capabilities.

BACHMAN INFORMATION SYSTEMS, INC. Bachman Information Systems, Inc. is exhibiting The Bachman Product Set, which supports the development of new applications while supporting existing applications. It provides the powerful maintenance, enhancement, and migration capabilities MIS departments need to control the largest component of their workload.

CATALYST CATALYST, an information technology firm of Peat Marwick, will present PATHVU, RETROFIT, ReACT, and DataTEC. PATHVU provides analysis and detailed reporting of program logic and structure. RETROFIT restructures Cobol code. ReACT translates Assembler programs to structured Cobol. DataTEC provides data element analysis, standardization, and migration capabilities. These products make up the reengineering baseline necessary to migrate existing systems to advanced technical environments.

Case Tools in Systems Design

CGI SYSTEMS, INC. PACBASE is a full-cycle CASE product. It integrates mainframe and PC-based analysis and designs workstations for the development and maintenance of application specifications. This is done through active prototypes, a centralized enterprisewide dictionary that controls and manages all business specifications directly into complete Cobol applications, including all code and documentation.

CHEN & ASSOCIATES, INC. Chen & Associates provides products, training, and consulting in data-oriented system development. Products (PC-based) are ER-Designer, which defines information requirements in entity-relationship diagrams; SCHEMAGEN, which generates schemas for your database systems (from micro-based to mainframe-based); Normalizer, which normalizes data or words.

COMPUTER SCIENCES CORP. The Technology Activity's Design Generator is an object-oriented expert system that automatically selects a central transform from a data-flow diagram and generates an initial design represented in structure chart notation. The graphic-intensive user interface features intelligent pop-up menus and multipane browsers.

CORTEX CORP. CorVision is an application development system that automates the entire software development cycle for the DEC VAX/VMS environment using a technique called Picture Programming. Picture Programming allows DP professionals to visualize an application by diagramming the design and then automatically generating a production-ready application directly from the pictures.

DIGITAL EQUIPMENT CORPORATION As a leading manufacturer, Digital provides a range of integrated application development tools for solutions to business and engineering problems. The offerings are workstation based and address all aspects of the Applications Development Life Cycle. They are integrated into the VAX hardware, software, and network architecture to provide enterprise wide solutions.

ETECH ALGORITHMS AND SYSTEMS, INC. ETECH SOFTROBOT is an intelligent workbench built on PSDDL (Problem Statement and Diagram Description Language). ETECH-D is a fully automatic diagramming toolkit without screen editing. ETECH-M is an intelligent project manager driven by Project-Makefile, ETECH-R is a reusing language, and ETECH-G is a language-independent code generator based on reusability. ETECH SOFTROBOT reaches many professionals' goals.

HOLLAND SYSTEMS CORP./DELOITTE HASKINS AND SELLS Deloitte Haskins and Sells and Holland Systems Corp. have pooled their proven consulting and software product expertise in the IRM area. The result is a line of products that address the entire information resource management process from business modeling to database design and analysis to application development and implementation. The companies will feature the 4Front Family of IRM products.

I-LOGIX, INC. I-Logix, Inc. pioneers system design automation with STATEMATE, the only available tool that models the dynamic behavior of real-time systems as well as system functions and architecture. With STATEMATE, users produce a specification that is compiled allowing its execution to be viewed on screen. STATEMATE includes three graphic languages for modeling, execution, and simulation capability; rapid prototyping in Ada; and 2167A documentation.

INDEX TECHNOLOGY Index Technology markets the Excelerator family of products that automate systems development. Products include PC PRism for systems planning, Excelerator and Excelerator/RTS for analysis and design, plus links to application generators and programming environments. Excelerator and Excelerator/RTS support a variety of techniques and methodologies and can be tailored for each organization's needs.

INFODYNE INTERNATIONAL, INC. InfoDyne, Inc. markets and distributes MASTER, a PC-based CASE tool and methodology, based on the E-R (entity-relationship) approach to systems planning and design. MASTER accommodates numerous approaches to the problem of analysis, design, and documentation of all design activities relating to the conceptual, logical, and physical model of data and international processes in an information system.

INFOREM PLC Inforem's Professional Application Generation Environment (PAGE) is a unique CASE offering. A multiuser product, it combines onscreen graphics with a systems encyclopedia and uses a relational database on networked PCs. PAGE is based on the Inforem method, which provides a seamless transition right from analysis to program code both for PC and mainframe systems.

INTEGRATED SYSTEMS, INC. AutoCode focuses on the needs of real-time software engineers and addresses all steps from analysis to design, stimulation and code generation. The graphical specification environment features engineering block diagrams, data flow/control flow, state transition, and process descriptions. Ward-Mellor real-time software methodology with Boeing-Hatley extensions are included in an environment where simulation and analysis can be performed for design verification; and real-time code in C, Ada, or Fortran can be generated automatically.

INTERACTIVE DEVELOPMENT ENVIRONMENT (IDE) IDE's product, Software through Pictures, is a set of integrated graphical editors and error-checking tools supporting structured analysis and design methods. The editors are linked to a data dictionary—supporting definition of names, types, constants, and associated text. Users can generate Ada declarations and define process and module templates to generate specifications.

JAMES MARTIN ASSOCIATES James Martin Associates, and international consulting firm established by James Martin, is considered the leader in creating systems development methods and CASE tools to support those methods. With more than 250 professionals throughout the world, JMA's teams provide commercial and government clients with technical and management services.

KNOWLEDGEWARE, INC. Knowledgeware, Inc. provides a complete integrated computer-aided software engineering (I-CASE) environment for the planning, analysis, design, construction and maintenance of computer-based information systems. The information engineering workbench (IEW) provides enterprise modeling, data modeling, process modeling, systems design, and code generation experts. The "Knowledge-Coordinator.Encyclopedia" team uses state-of-the-art artificial intelligence technology.

LANGUAGE TECHNOLOGY Language Technology provides CASE products to the IBM mainframe market. The company's flagship product RECODER is the leading Cobol structuring tool. RECODER automatically transforms difficult to maintain, unstructured Cobol into structured Cobol. Language Technology's INSPECTOR is the only quality assurance tool based on scientific measurement of Cobol quality and maintainability.

AGEMENT SYSTEMS, INC. LBMS will present its PC-based tools, SUPER-MATE and AUTO-MATE PLUS. SUPER-MATE provides a powerful set of automated facilities for strategic planning, including business area/activity analysis, analysis of competitive strategies, the prioritization of applications, and the development of the strategic plan. Results of this plan may be passed to AUTO-MATE PLUS, which provides full support for systems analysis, logical design and automatic generation of physical designs and data dictionary syntax for ADABAS, DB2, and other DBMS.

MANAGER SOFTWARE PRODUCTS (MSP) The MANAGER family of products (PC and mainframe) is dedicated to automating all phases of the systems life cycle, from strategic information planning to the generation of enabled code. MSP will present managerVIEW, the intelligent workstation-based graphical information engineering tool driven by the central knowledge base resident on the corporate dictionary. ManagerVIEW is integrated with the mainframe corporate dictionary and also runs on the IBM PC family and PS/2.

MICHAEL JACKSON SYSTEMS, LTD. Jackson CASE tools automate the widely acclaimed Michael Jackson methods of system development and program design. SPEED-BUILDER supports the analysis phase of development through powerful graphical and text facilities and automates documentation production. The cooperating program development facility (PDF) generates complete, well-structured program code from Jackson structure charts.

MICRO FOCUS Micro Focus Cobol/2 Workbench puts a mainframe programming and testing environment on a PC platform under MS-DOS or OS/2. It is used by developers of Cobol, CICS DL/I, and IMS DB/DC applications to improve productivity and cut applications development backlogs. Micro Focus Cobol compilers and CASE tools are the choice of IBM, AT&T, Sun Microsystems, Microsoft, and others.

NASTEC CORP. Nastec Corporation develops tools for commercial, government, and engineering software developers. CASE 2000 DesignAid is based upon an interactive, multiuser database with features for process modeling, real-time system modeling, and documentation. Operating in the IBM PC and Digital VAX environment, CASE 2000 also includes tools for requirements management, project management and control, and consulting and training in CASE technology.

NETRON, INC. The NETRON/CAP Development Center is a CASE system for building custom, portable Cobol software using a frame-based software engineering process called Bassett Frame Technology. NETRON/CAP unifies the prototyping/development/maintenance life cycle into an automated specification procedure. The open design architecture allows unlimited automation of additional application functionality for IBM mainframes and PCs, VAX systems, and Wang VS minis.

OPTIMA, INC. (Formerly known as Ken Orr & Associates) Optima, Inc. integrates the use of tools and technology with the experience of people. DSSd (data structured systems development), the flagship product, is a life-cycle methodology which serves as the base of the product offering. CASE tool products which automate the methodology are Brackets, for the diagramming process, and Design-Machine, for requirements definition and logical database design.

ON-LINE SOFTWARE INTERNATIONAL On-Line Software International presents CasePac Automated Software Development with a powerful DB2 data dictionary. As the foundation for On-Line Software's CASE platform, CasePac provides a complete, fully active central repository, software engineering facilities including a graphics front end, change management, and maintenance facilities.

PANSOPHIC SYSTEMS, INC. Pansophic Systems Inc. presents TELON. The TELON application development system captures design specifications to generate Cobol or DL/I applications. TELON assists the transition from analysis to design by providing interfaces to leading front end analysis tools. TELON components include directory, data administration, screen/report painters, prototyping, specification facilities, automated documentation, generator, and test facility.

POLYTRON CORP. POLYTRON offers the leading configuration management system for MS/DOSPC and VAX/VMS software development. PVCS maintains versions and revisions of software systems. PolyMake automatically rebuilds any desired version of the system. PolyLibrarian maintains libraries of reusable object modules. The tools work together or independently with *any* language and your existing tools.

POPKIN SOFTWARE & SYSTEMS, INC. Popkin Software & Systems offers SYSTEM ARCHITECT, a PC-based CASE tool running under

Microsoft Windows. Its set of process and data driven methodologies for structured analysis and design include DeMarco/Yourdon, Gane and Sarson, Ward & Mellor (real-time), structure charts, and entity-relationship diagrams. SYSTEM ARCHITECTS'S Data Dictionary-Encyclopedia utilizes the dBASE II file format.

READY SYSTEMS Ready Systems will present CARDTools, which supports automatic DoD 2167 documentation generation, specific Ada requirements, including object-oriented design, packages, information hiding, and rendezvous. CARDTools offers real-time performance deadline analysis on multitasking architectures, and hardware/software interface specification, including intertasking synchronization and communication designs, allowing for design analysis verification prior to actual implementation.

SAGE SOFTWARE, INC. Sage Software, Inc. develops, markets, and supports a family of CASE tools for developers of IBM-based informations systems. The company's product family (known as the APS Development Center) encompasses the software development cycle and supports the physical design, interactive prototyping, coding, testing, and maintenance of Cobol-based applications software.

SOFTLAB, INC. Softlab, Inc. will present MAESTRO, the integrated Software Engineering Environment. MAESTRO organizes, manages the software cycle through real-time project management, time accounting, and your standards. MAESTRO integrates customizable tools for design, coding, testing, documentation, and maintenance, is language independent, and fits in numerous hardware and software environments.

TEKTRONIX TekCASE is a family of automated software development tools that help software engineers and project managers analyze, design, document, manage, and maintain complex real-time systems. Because they support Digital's complete VAX line and integrate with VAXset software, Tekcase products are flexible, extensible, and especially well suited for large projects.

TEXAS INSTRUMENTS Texas Instruments' integrated CASE product, The Information Engineering Facility, is designed to automate the complete systems development life cycle. It consists of a powerful mainframe encyclopedia and PC-based, graphical toolsets to support analysis and design. TI can demonstrate today the major components of this product including strategic planning, analysis, design, Cobol code and database generation.

THE CADWARE GROUP, LTD. The CADWARE Group, Ltd. designs, produces, and markets rule-based frameworks and modeling tools for development of complex systems. Managers, planners, systems analysts, and designers use these tools to help manage the complexity of defining and evaluating mission-critical business, industrial, and technical systems.

TRANSFORM LOGIC CORP. Transform addresses the development and maintenance of the entire application life cycle. Using expert system technology, complete Cobol applications are produced for IBM mainframe DBMSs DL/I and DB2. The concepts behind automated development, data driven design architecture, prototyping, and maintenance are reviewed with examples of user accomplishments.

VISUAL SOFTWARE, INC. Visual Software, Inc. markets personal CASE tools for workstations, LAN, and mainframe design environments. The base package, vsDesigner, is a methodology-independent workbench supporting shared access to LAN-based information repositories. Several default design syntaxes come with the product, including those for real-time design. Extensive analyses are supported and an optional SQL interface to the design data is available.

YOURDON, INC. The YOURDON Analyst/Designer Toolkit supports both the traditional and real-time YOURDON Techniques and allows for the creation of all the diagrams associated with the techniques. The diagramming facilities of the Toolkit are integrated with a powerful project dictionary which features dBase III compatibility. The Toolkit provides error checking to ensure the accuracy of diagrams and dictionary entries.

11.6 Getting CASE in Place

There are three basic steps for implementing CASE technology in a software development organization:

- Determine methodology and automation support requirements
- Select a CASE product
- Implement the CASE product

This is a lengthy process involving numerous people, so do not expect major results for a couple of years. Even then, the biggest and longest-term benefits may come in application maintenance. CASE tools make it much easier to maintain specifications.

11.6.1   Determine the Methodology

Following agreement on the organization methodology, whether dataflow or entity-relationship diagrams, your next step is what you need most in automation support. For a larger organization, with complex applications, you may want some of the following capabilities:

- Interactive drawing of analysis diagrams
- Automatic date normalization
- Consistency checking
- Initialization of physical design from requirements
- Prototyping tools
- Directory of reusable code modules
- Analysis methodology enforcements
- Interface with application development environment

A second key decision is whether you want a single integrated environment or a CASE front-end to a more classical development environment.

11.6.2   Select a CASE Product

Once you have determined your methodology and decided that CASE capabilities will be useful, you need to select a product. You may do this on the basis of:

- What environment — PC or mainframe?
- What application does the tool support — some tools support a specific database; e.g., DB2, or language; e.g., Ada?
- Does the tool support your methodology?
- Is the vendor financially secure? — You may want to talk to people who have experience using the vendor's CASE tool.

11.6.3   Implement the CASE Product

An aggressive strategy for CASE implementation in smaller organizations is to automate many software engineering techniques simultaneously on a small trial project. The basic steps are as follows:

- Select a new development project to be used for the CASE trial situation.
- Staff the trial project with your best requirements and design analysts.
- Assign a full-time CASE administrator to learn the tool, make detailed methodology decisions, enter information, run analysis reports, and generate specifications.

A large organization with thousands of users nationwide must take a different approach. Most such organizations find it physically impossible to decide on a complete automated methodology and then get hundreds of people trained on it in a short time period.

In this circumstance, a method or support group acts as change agent, introducing a few techniques at a time and supporting them with automation.

11.7   Conclusion

This chapter introduced a tool that has literally taken the software development world by storm. CASE tools are making a big impact in software development and will continue to do so for years to tome. This chapter showed how they could be selected and used in small or large organizations.

12

Disaster Recovery

Introduction

This chapter discusses an aspect of information resource management that is very often overlooked by the data processing industry. Disaster recovery is very seldom considered when organizations discuss the planning for, managing, and controlling of the information resource.

This chapter deals with disaster recovery: the plans and procedures that should be in place in order to assist an organization in recovery from a disaster; the testing and execution of those plans and procedures; the personnel required to execute those plans; and the actions required during the disaster.

12.1 What Is a Disaster?

A disaster may be defined as a threat to which an organization is vulnerable. The threat may be classified as accidental or intentional. Disasters are sometimes classified as natural (acts of God) or man-made (perpetrated by man).

The categories of disasters that pose a threat to the organization's information resource and the ones that will be discussed in this chapter are:

- Fires
- Floods
- Earthquakes
- Hostage situations
- Power loss
- Wind storms
- Snow or ice storms
- Equipment failure

12.2 What Is a Disaster Recovery Plan?

A disaster recovery plan may be defined as a document that indicates the steps or actions to be taken by an organization, if struck by a disaster, to declare a disaster, continue processing information during the period of the disaster, and render the information processing facility operable in a manner equivalent to before the disaster occurred. Actions will need to be taken in respect to:

- Personnel
- Equipment
- Supplies
- Suppliers
- Systems and programs
- Stored data

The next several sections discuss the various components of disaster recovery planning.

12.3 The Disaster Recovery Team

The overall function of the disaster recovery team is to undertake the various tasks that will allow an organization to continue its operational activities and recover its operation once a disaster has been declared.

The composition, functions, and responsibilities of the recovery team are as follows:

TEAM MEMBER	TITLE/FUNCTION
Team Coordinator	Heads the team and chairs regular sessions of the team during a disaster.
Primary Site Restoration Coordinator	Heads the group charged with the restoration of the primary site.
Recovery Site Coordinator	Heads the group charged with preparing the recovery site and processing at that site.
Disaster Notification Coordinator	Responsible for notifying all personnel of a disaster.
Management/Administration Coordinator	Responsible for reporting all management/administration decisions to recovery team during a disaster and keeping management appraised of recovery efforts.
Application/User Coordinator	Responsible for group charged with the processing and maintenance of critical applications during a disaster and keeping users appraised of recovery efforts.
Systems Software Coordinator	Responsible for group charged with the generation and maintenance of the operating system and all attendant software at the recovery site during a disaster.
Communications Coordinator	Responsible for the group charged with the generation of control programs and maintenance of all communications equipment during a disaster.
Hardware/Operations Coordinator	Responsible for the group charged with operating all hardware at the recovery site and production and distribution of reports and outputs to the organization during a disaster.
Command Site Coordinator	Responsible for selecting, equipping, and operating a site from which the recovery team will operate during a disaster.

The recovery team will use the following tools and deliverables:

1. Tools used by recovery team

   - Critical supplies list
   - Suppliers/Salesman list
   - Disaster notification list
   - List of items stored off-site
   - Equipment inventory list
   - List of critical programs

2. Deliverables from the recovery team session

   - Decision to process at recovery site or delay processing until restoration of primary site
   - Level of service plan
   - Security requirements list
   - Schedule for running production jobs and recovery site
   - Transportation requirements

12.4 Review Data Center Operations

The review of the data center operations is the main data collection phase of the disaster recovery study. It allows the recovery team to determine the hardware/software configuration of the center and to examine what documents exist in the following areas:

AREAS	DOCUMENTS
Hardware Configuration	Diagrams, layouts, or maps of the hardware and inventory lists.
Operating System Environment	Operating System (e.g., MVS, DOS/VSE) including version or level numbers; TP monitors (CICS or VOLLIE) including version or level numbers; modems; controllers; and number of terminals.
Number of Operating Hours and Day of Operations	Usage charts or diagrams showing hours the system is up per day and days per week. These documents are useful in selecting a backup site.

AREAS	DOCUMENTS
Operation of Input/Output Areas	Documents showing distribution of reports. The recovery team should examine the I/O areas to evaluate the security of stored reports and printed sensitive information (e.g., payroll checks) and the retrieval of reports or printed information from holding bins.
Physical and Data Security	Documented procedures for allowing access to the computer room. The recovery team should examine logon procedures, authentication codes, and general protection mechanisms.
Scheduling of Critical and Noncritical Jobs	The recovery team should examine existing scheduling documents to evaluate job mixes, run cycles, and priorities of major jobs.
Existing Disaster Recovery Plans	The recovery team should examine all documents relating to disaster recovery and any recovery action plans.

12.5 Review Current Backup and Restore Procedures

The purpose is to determine and evaluate how the organization currently backs up and restores its data files, teleprocessing monitors, and source libraries.

The recovery team will examine procedures in the following areas:

- Backup of CICs
- Backup of VSAM files or other databases
- Backup of online and batch source libraries

This phase will seek to determine what utilities are used to back up the above listed items, how often the items are backed up, and how many copies are kept on-site and sent off-site.

The recovery team will also evaluate the existing backup and restore procedures and make recommendations.

12.6   Review Current Off-Site Storage Procedures

The purpose of this phase is to examine and evaluate existing procedures at the organization's data center for transporting and storing backup copies of files at off-site locations.

The scope of the phase includes examining existing logs recording identification of backup files, version of backup, and date of backup.

The recovery team will examine the logs for signatures required to send files to the off-site storage and receipt of older versions of backup files back at the data center.

The primary determination of this phase is how stored materials will be retrieved from the off-site location during a disaster. The recovery team will examine evidence that access (by phone) can be obtained to the off-site location during nonbusiness hours and that particular versions or generations of backup files can be easily obtained during the disaster.

The recovery team will also determine the security and authentication procedures in place to maintain the integrity of the organization's data at all times. It should be established that only authorized personnel can retrieve files, at all times, from the off-site location.

12.7   Identify and Rank Critical Applications

This is the most important phase of the study. It is from this phase that the recovery team obtains criteria that are useful in determining the adequacy of the recovery site.

During this phase, the team establishes the following:

- Data collection methods for all applications that will be processed during the disaster. The team determines cut-off times for collecting this data and what other jobs are dependent on the successful collection of this data.
- The maximum allowable downtime during which the application can remain unprocessed without having a detrimental impact on the users.
- How source documents will be retained and used to regenerate files that may be destroyed for which there is no backup. For example, how will online data be recaptured if a disaster occurred between scheduled backups.
- The maximum level of service that will be acceptable to the users during the disaster and recovery periods. The team will determine

what changes in processing frequency, number of online terminals, number of reports, and types of reports are acceptable.
- The priority of jobs and what jobs will be processed during the disaster.
- The minimum number of support staff, operators of terminals and printers, disk storage devices, and controllers that will be required to keep the applications going.

The recovery team will develop surveys to collect data which will allow for the identifying and ranking of the critical applications and services.

12.8   Identify Critical Suppliers

The purpose of this phase is to produce a comprehensive inventory of supplies and suppliers. The inventory will include:

- Identification of critical supplies and suppliers
- Contacts within suppliers (including phone numbers during business and nonbusiness hours)
- Departments responsible for order and reorder of supplies
- Location of temporary storage of supplies (partial amounts to keep a processing cycle going)
- Lead times for obtaining critical supplies

The importance of this phase cannot be overemphasized. The ability to recover from a disaster and the time to recover is dependent on the availability of critical supplies.

The phase will also collect information on unique equipment that is critical to the recovery effort. This includes:

- Signature plates
- Microfiche or film readers
- MICR machines
- 96-column card readers

12.9   Review Backup Site

During this phase, the recovery team will review the backup site and determine whether the site can support the minimum requirements of the organization in the following areas:

- Operating System
- Data Storage
- Online and Batch Processing
- Physical and Data Security

The recovery team will seek to determine that the recovery site either has a native operating system (e.g., MVS, DOS/VSE) or can simulate (using VM) a compatible operating system for use by the data center during the disaster. The system (through its resident program) must be able to support any "fixes" that are required to run the critical programs of the center and allow for critical backup and recovery of all data.

The recovery site must be able to support the data storage requirements of the data center. If storage media are not identical, then (through software) it must allow for that storage, for example, storage of data on 3350 disk on 3380 disk and vice versa.

The site must be able to support the minimum amount of terminals, controllers, and printers required by the center. The recovery team will ensure that all security requirements for physical and data security, report distribution and storage, and access to computer and work areas are met by the recovery site.

12.10   Define Scope of Disaster Recovery Study

The purpose of this phase of the study is to set the scope of the disaster recovery action plan. The action plan is a step-by-step account of actions that must be taken by the organization's data center and user personnel to recover from a declared disaster.

The actions taken by the data center are determined to a large extent by the magnitude of destruction of the computing facilities.

The recovery team will interview recommended personnel at the data center to determine whether the plan should be written for total or partial destruction of the computer facilities.

The recovery team will deliver, at the end of the study, a comprehensive document detailing activities that must be undertaken at the center and in the affected departments to declare a disaster, notify all critical individuals, secure the damaged site after insurance assessment, move processing to the recovery site, and rebuild the damaged primary site.

12.11 Develop Inventory Procedures

This phase outlines procedures that the organization must adhere to in order to develop a comprehensive list of suppliers.

The deliverable from this phase is used for two reasons: (1) insurance — to make a claim after a disaster, and (2) replacement — to determine what was lost or stolen and must be replaced.

The results of this phase will be a document showing what is available, who holds the item, how it can be ordered, and any substantive identifying information about the item.

12.12 Develop Backup Site Capabilities

The purpose of this phase is to develop, test, and make available a backup site at which the organization can process its data while the primary site is being restored following a disaster. The primary deliverable from this phase will be a site compatible with the current site of the organization. The recovery team will undertake the following tasks during this phase:

- Generate a compatible operating system at the backup site. The operating system can be run in either a native mode (e.g., MVS, DOS/VSE) or be simulated using a VM-like operating system.
- Load all existing data for critical applications onto storage devices at the backup site. These include VSAM files, databases, source libraries, load modules, and all required utilities.
- Test the ability to retrieve data, back up and restore the data, and support all requirements for printing and displaying that data.
- Generate a telecommunications system that will support the online processing requirements of the primary site. This will include NCP generation, loading, and compiling of source programs for CICS and any other TP monitors that are required. The recovery team will ensure that the required number of ports are available to support online terminals and that controllers and control programs are all tested and in working order.
- Compile, debug, and test critical applications that will be processed at the recovery site. The recovery team will ensure that all programs, including those with nonstandard "fixes" and "patches," can be processed at the recovery site.
- Run all core applications and make results available to the data center and users for comparison with results from the primary site.

The recovery team will turn over a complete documentation package for this phase of the project, including procedures for maintaining the software and applications at the recovery site.

12.13   Develop and Test a Recovery Plan

The purpose of this phase is to develop and test a comprehensive disaster recovery action plan. The action plan is a step-by-step account of actions that must be taken by the organization's data center staff and user personnel to process data during a disaster and restore the primary site.

The action plan will include information on the following topics:

• Activities by user departments
• Disaster notification list
• Disaster recovery activities
• Vital areas of recovery
• Telecommunications requirements
• Primary and recovery site security
• Plan testing and maintenance
• Alternate processing approaches

During this phase, the organization's data center and user departments will be broken down into various activity areas for the purpose of effecting the disaster recovery plan and meeting the stated objectives of the plan.

The activity areas are better defined as areas in which certain disaster recovery-related activities are conducted to effect recovery of the primary site and data processing at the recovery site. For example, the data center may be broken down into the following activity areas:

• Management/Administration
• Systems Programming
• Applications Programming
• Production Scheduling and Operations
• User Department Services
• Equipment Manufacturer Services
• Transportation
• Recovery Team Services
• Data Processing Steering Committee

The activities of the management/administration activity area include:

- Coordinate restoration effort at the primary site
- Coordinate retrieval of vital items from various off-site storage locations and delivery to the recovery site
- Schedule the production of jobs based on priorities established when critical applications were identified and ranked
- Monitor and backup and recovery procedures during the disaster period
- Monitor the service levels during the disaster period

The recovery team should develop a list of personnel who should be notified when a disaster occurs. The list will include persons within and outside the organization. Those persons outside the organization will include police, fire department, equipment suppliers, and insurance representatives.

The comprehensive action plan will include activities that must be carried out at the primary and recovery sites during the disaster period.

The activities at the primary site will include:

- Disaster declaration
- Disaster notification
- Damage assessment by insurance agent
- Vital items retrieval
- Site cleanup
- Physical security maintenance
- Repair/Replace equipment and computer room
- Load and test operating system and application programs
- Backup of vital items
- Backup and restoration of input transactions
- Replace missing documentation and procedure manuals

The recovery team must identify items and vital areas within the organization that must be recovered and placed in a ready status to effect the disaster recovery action plan. During this phase, the team will identify vital functions, procedures, and reports that must be preserved in each user department to assist in the recovery.

The recovery team will determine the telecommunications needs of the organization during this phase. The requirements will not be limited to the number of modems or controllers that will be required to keep the data center functional but will examine modifications that may be required. These modifications may include:

- Modifying VTAM books to define the terminals and printers at the recovery site

- Modifying VTAM books for remote terminals to incorporate various macros used by NCP
- Cataloging VTAM books in the Source Statement Library
- Including VTAM books in start-up books for VTAM
- LINKediting the assembled NCP statements

The recovery team will evaluate and document in the action plan the security requirements at the primary and recovery sites. The evaluation should not be limited to physical security but should also include data security considerations.

In the area of data security, the recovery team should evaluate the threats to which the data center is exposed and the existing protection mechanisms in place to counter those threats. The team will determine the adequacy of existing protection mechanisms and recommend further protection if the situation warrants it.

12.13.1 Test of the Disaster Recovery Action Plan

The recovery team should conduct tests of the disaster recovery action plan to ensure that:

- The plan is complete and workable.
- The materials and data are available and usable to perform alternate processing for critical applications.
- The system and library files and application software are current and processable.
- Processing can be resumed as planned.

The plan should be tested at three levels:

- Level 1 — Adequacy of off-site storage of files and documentation.
- Level 2 — Capability to restore the primary site using off-site files and documentation.
- Level 3 — Capability of producing a comparable operating system and processing environment at the recovery site.
  The areas to be tested will include:
- Backup for

  — VSAM files
  — Databases
  — JCL
  — Operating system

- Documentation backup for

  — Operations
  — Operating system
  — Applications
  — User procedures

- Supplies backup for

  — Special forms
  — Preprinted forms
  — Input documents

The recovery team should assist the organization's data center in conducting simulated disasters and "fire drill" tests. These tests may be as simple as bringing down the entire computer system, without prior notice, and restoring it from tapes and files stored off-site to full-scale tests with all areas, including user departments, involved.

The team will develop procedures to enable the data center to keep the action plan current; make additions, deletions, or revisions as the situation warrants; and monitor the performance of the plan in areas such as:

- Ability to generate a compatible system at the primary site from stored off-site data.
- Ability to retrieve items from off-site locations.
- Ability to run online and batch programs at the recovery site.
- Ability to update hardware and software at recovery site.
- Ability to back up critical personnel.
- Ability to evaluate required security features at both the recovery and primary sites.

12.14   Data Collection for Disaster Recovery Plan

The data that constitutes the disaster recovery plan is collected, primarily through surveys, from all functional areas of the organization. The surveys are constructed so as to obtain information on the organization's business functions, critical personnel, supplies, potential loss due to a disaster, ability to remain functioning during and after a disaster, and technology requirements.

Exhibits A and B illustrate two questionnaires developed to collect business function and data processing information:

EXHIBIT A
QUESTIONNAIRE TO DETERMINE
BUSINESS FUNCTIONS
(DISASTER RECOVERY ACTION PLAN)

1. List the business functions critical to the operation of your department.

2. List the functions in your department that are related to the processing of computerized data.

3. List all employees who perform critical functions in your departments and are vital to the corporation's disaster recovery effort.

4. List all supplies (both computer and noncomputer) critical to the operating of your department.

5. In the event of a disaster, what functions must be performed in order for the department to survive and recover?

6. List all vital items in your department that should be stored off-site.

7. In the event of a disaster, what activities must be conducted in your department that will allow MIS to recover the primary site?

8. In the event of a disaster, what activities must be conducted in your department that will allow MIS to process data at the recovery site?

9. What will be the transportation needs for relocation of personnel, movement of data and reports, and conveyance of vital documents during a disaster?

10. What level of protection and security will be required for your transportation needs during a disaster?

11. List all critical reports that must be produced by MIS for your department during a disaster.

12. List all personnel within and outside of your department who should be notified about a disaster.

13. List all personnel critical to your department survival to whom a copy of the disaster recovery plan should be given.

14. List, in order of priority, all critical reports you must have produced by MIS to survive a disaster.

15. Indicate off-site storage of all vital items and how they can be retrieved during a disaster.

16. In the event of a disaster, what is the critical number of terminals that must be located at the recovery site to support your department?

17. Who are the critical people who will be required to operate these terminals?

18. In the event of a disaster, how would you capture and record data that is now entered online into the computer system?

19. If the online system is down for several days, would MIS have to produce any special reports for you that they are not now providing?

20. Are you now contracted to produce any reports for other departments or parties by specific dates and times?

21. Are there any legal filings of specific reports to federal government agencies or other government agencies that must be adhered to during a disaster?

22. Indicate monetary loss to your department if you could not process data for:

    (a) 10–20 hours
    (b) 1–2 days
    (c) 3–5 days
    (d) 6–10 days

EXHIBIT B
QUESTIONNAIRE TO DETERMINE DP NEEDS
(DISASTER RECOVERY ACTION PLAN)

1. List all equipment (including model numbers) at the primary site.

2. List all suppliers (including salesman/number) for the primary site.

3. List the location(s) of off-site storage and how items can be retrieved during an emergency.

4. List procedures to be followed to declare a disaster and move to an off-site facility.

5. List procedures to be followed to declare a disaster and restore the primary site.

6. Indicate how physical security will be maintained during a disaster.

7. Indicate what operating system and program testing will be done after recovery of the primary site.

8. List all vital items required to recover the primary site (assuming total shutdown).

9. List all critical personnel required to recover the primary site.

10. List any unique requirements for any equipment at the primary site.

11. Indicate how vital items backup will be done during the disaster.

12. List all personnel who will be notified of a disaster at the primary site.

13. Indicate how items not backed up will be reconstructed and added to the input for the primary site recovery.

12.15   Synopsis of Disaster Recovery Activities

There is a cycle of activities that an organization must go through to declare and recover from a disaster. That cycle was discussed in detail in this chapter. In summary, those activities are as follows:

- Recovery team reports to command center
- Coordinator notifies the insurance adjuster
- Notification coordinator notifies all personnel
- Insurance adjuster examines site
- Recovery team examines site
- Manufacturers' representative examines site
- Representative presents outage report to recovery team
- Recovery team makes an inventory of items
- Recovery team decides to remain at primary site or process at recovery site
- Notify recovery team of disaster
- Order vital supplies
- Retrieve vital items from off-site storage
- Prepare recovery site
- Coordinate movement of staff to recovery site
- Notify staff of alternate duties
- Suspend all application development and maintenance
- Move needed supplies to recovery site
- Load operating system at recovery site
- Load production programs and data files
- Hook up terminals
- Run scheduled production jobs at recovery site

12.16   Summary

This chapter discussed all aspects of disaster recovery in some detail. The various phases of a disaster recovery plan were highlighted, although in no particular order. A complete disaster recovery plan is described in the appendices.

12.5 Synopsis of Disaster Recovery Activities

There is a great deal of activity that goes into disaster recovery. In order to give you a picture from a distance, Table 12.5 below describes, in detail in this chapter. In summary, these activities are:

* Detect the event and notify the concerned parties
* Configure facilities for alternate objects
* Notify appropriate and relevant personnel
* Account for all personnel
* Inventory damage, resume, etc.
* Take emergency actions
* Manage assets (inspection for each that site)
* Represent individuals out to appropriate recovery team
* Implement plans for inventory or items
* Regain control over the critical resources or property at alternate sites
* Settle communications of members in
* Order supplies
* Locate vital records from affected offices
* Deploy response teams
* Coordinate movement of staff to recovery site
* Inventory all of alternate facilities
* Implement applications environment and maintenance
* Manage data handling; recovery site
* Coordinate processing at recovery site
* Load application program and data, etc.
* Test applications
* Perform initial processing, etc. at recovery site

12.6 Summary

This chapter addressed a variety of disaster recovery in active detail. The central message of this chapter is every plan must be implemented, tested and maintained to be viable. Even with the best preparations, plan for effective interruptions.

An Implementable Disaster Recovery Plan

The plan presented here was developed by the author and implemented in its entirety at a Health Maintenance Organization (HMO).

APPROACH TO DISASTER RECOVERY:
AN IMPLEMENTABLE PLAN

TABLE OF CONTENTS

10.0 Vital Areas of Recovery

- Records
- User Department
- MIS Department
- Operations System
- Software Package
- Applications
- Off-site Storage

11.0 Equipment Inventory
12.0 Telecommunications Requirements
13.0 Sites Security
14.0 Plan Testing
15.0 Plan Maintenance
16.0 Off-site Storage Requirement
17.0 Preventive Measures

17.1 Introduction
17.2 Component Failure Analysis
17.3 Risk Assessment
17.4 Protection Mechanisms
17.5 System Outage Analysis

18.0 Disaster Recovery Forms

APPENDIX A

1.   Process at Comdisco with North and South Offices
2.   Process at Comdisco with North Office
3.   Process at Comdisco with South Office
4.   Process at Comdisco with Ready Area

APPENDIX B

1.   Transportation Needs
2.   Reports Distribution Plan
3.   Office Space Requirements
4.   Schedule of Jobs by Priority

APPENDIX C

1.   Disaster Plan Distribution List
2.   List of Critical Reports

3.   Priority of Critical Programs
4.   Critical Employees

APPENDIX D

1.   Critical Supplies List
2.   Security Requirements
3.   Critical Number of Terminals
4.   Special Reports
5.   Contracted for Reports

APPENDIX E

1.   Generating and Operating System at Comdisco
2.   Changes to Primary Site Operating System

1.0 Introduction

This document describes the HealthWays Disaster Recovery Plan in considerable detail.

The major objectives of the disaster recovery plan are to:

• Restore the primary site following a major outage
• Continue processing of company data at a recovery site while restoration is in progress

While the intent of the plan is to prevent any loss of company data if a security breach or disaster occurs, the scope of the plan is to enable HealthWays to recover from a total shutdown or outage of the computer facility. Thus, the plan will include descriptions of all the procedures and vital items that are necessary to enable recovery from a total outage of the computer facility.

The plan is written in several sections, as indicated by the table of contents.

The recovery team section lists the teams and their functions. The major functions of the teams are:

1.   Notify relevant parties if a disaster is declared.
2.   Restore the primary site.
3.   Generate the operating system at the recovery site.
4.   Manage the installation at the recovery site for the period of the disaster.

5. Manage the recovery effort at the recovery site.
6. Run the production jobs at the recovery site.

The activity areas section lists the departments in HealthWays that will contribute to the restoration of the primary site and the continued processing of company data at the recovery site.

The activity list section describes all the activities that must take place in the various departments and at the primary and recovery sites to meet the objectives of the disaster recovery plan.

The disaster notification section lists the names, affiliation, recovery responsibility, and phone numbers of all personnel who should be contacted after a disaster. The lists include major manufacturers, suppliers, salesmen, and personnel within and outside the company who should be notified in the event of a disaster.

The disaster recovery activities section describes the activities that must be conducted at both the primary and recovery sites to meet the objectives of the recovery plan.

The vital areas recovery section describes the vital items in each area that must either be reconstructed or retrieved from off-site storage to be used in the recovery effort at the primary site or data processing effort at the recovery site.

The equipment inventory section lists the major equipment, model number, and manufacturers of the equipment held by HealthWays Systems, Inc.

The telecommunications requirements section describes all the equipment, modems, controllers, and their configuration that are required to support HealthWays online data processing needs and CICS both at the primary and recovery sites.

The sites security section describes the security in place, the security requirements, and disaster preventive measures existing at both the primary and recovery sites.

The plan testing section describes how the plan will be tested at both the primary and the recovery sites. At the recovery site, the test will include the ability to generate an operating system and run production jobs. At the primary site, the test will include the ability to simulate a disaster producing a total outage and recover from the outage.

The plan maintenance section describes how the various departments will update the various sections of the plan. The plan should be updated at least once per year.

The off-site storage requirement section lists the items that are stored off-site, the department that stored the item, the location of the facility, and the 24-hour phone contact of the facility.

The preventive measures section indicates the measures that HealthWays can implement to lessen the impact of a disaster or prevent a disaster. The measures include conducting risk assessment, analysis of component failure and system outages, and the installation of protection mechanisms.

The final section lists the number and types of forms used to implement the recovery plan.

2.0 The Disaster Recovery Team

2.1 Introduction

This section describes the recovery team, its composition, administration, and the tools used by the team.

2.2 Composition of Recovery Team

The recovery team will consist of the following members:

Member	Title/Responsibility
Jay Ruparel	Systems Programmer
Denis Roy	Computer Operator
Simon Baskerville	Computer Operator
Patricia Akellian	Primary Site Restoration Coordinator
Kathy Schefter	Disaster Notification Production Scheduling
Thomas Tiernan	Primary Site Restoration
Joseph Grieco	Primary Site Restoration Coordinator Recovery Site Processing
Steve Markowitz	Coordinate all disaster recovery activities-user departments
Alternate Member	Title/Responsibility
Chuck Miller	Primary Site Restoration
Charlene Abrams	Primary Site Restoration Recovery Site Processing

Member	Title/Responsibility
External Member	Title/Responsibility
External Consultant	Provide Recovery Expertise

2.3 Recovery Team Administration and Functions

The following paragraphs describe the administration of the recovery team and the major functions it performs.

The administration of the recovery team is as follows:

Title	Major Function
Coordinator	Heads the team and chairs regular sessions during a disaster
Primary Site Restoration Coordinator	Heads the group charged with the restoration of the primary site
Recovery Site Coordinator	Heads the group charged with preparing the recovery site environment and processing at that site
Disaster Notification Coordinator	Responsible for notifying all personnel of a disaster
Operating Systems Specialist	Responsible for generation and maintenance of the operating system at the recovery site
Resource Pool Coordinator	Responsible for attracting external disaster recovery experts to serve on the recovery team

2.3.1 Recovery Team Functions

The functions of the recovery team can be placed in four categories:

• Management and disaster notification
• Primary site restoration
• Operating system generation and maintenance
• Recovery operations and running of production jobs

2.4 Tools and Deliverables of the Recovery Team

The following paragraphs describe the tools with which the team performs its duties and the deliverable from various meetings of the teams.

The tools the team uses are as follows:

1. Critical supplies list
2. Suppliers/salesmen list
3. Disaster notification list
4. List of items stored off-site
5. Equipment inventory list
6. List of critical programs, their priorities, and schedule
7. Office space requirements list
8. Outages due to disasters reporting form

The deliverables from the team sessions are:

1. Decision to process at recovery site or delay processing until restoration of primary site
2. Level of service plan
3. Security requirements list
4. Revised schedule for running production jobs at recovery site
5. Revised transportation requirements

3.0 Disaster Recovery Action Plan (Processing at Recovery Site)

3.1 Introduction

This section describes the actions that will be taken by HealthWays to recover from a total outage of data processing service due to a disaster and process at the recovery site.

3.2 Initial Report of a Disaster

The person who witnesses the occurrence of a disaster must first report it to the local authority and emergency services and then to the following people:

		Telephone	
Name	Function	Home	Office
Arnie Hanson	Building Manager		636-4211
S. Markowitz	Coordinator of HealthWays Disaster Recovery		636-6200 Ext. 260

3.3 Coordinator Reports to Command Center

The coordinator of disaster recovery will report to one of the following command centers:

Hotel	Location	Phone Number
1. Woodbridge Hilton	120 Wood Ave. So. Iselin, NJ 08830	494-6200
2. Landmark Inn	U.S. Route 1 & 9 Woodbridge, NJ 07095	636-2700

3.4 Recovery Team Reports to Command Center

The coordinator of disaster recovery will call all members of the recovery team and ask them to report to the designated command center.

The coordinator notifies all HealthWays executives and the data processing committee.

3.5 Coordinator Notifies the Insurance Adjusters

The coordinator will notify the insurance adjuster(s) of an occurrence of a disaster at HealthWays. It is important that no member of the recovery team or HealthWays employee enter the disaster site or examine any damaged equipment until the adjuster indicates it can be done. A failure to obey this directive may result in HealthWays being denied legitimate claims.

3.6 Disaster Notification Coordinator Notifies All Personnel on List

The disaster notification coordinator will notify all employees and nonemployees on the notification list of the occurrence of a disaster at HealthWays. All department heads will in turn notify their employees about reporting to work. Again, it is important to stress that no HealthWays employees be allowed into the affected areas before the insurance adjuster(s).

3.7 Insurance Adjuster Examines Site

The insurance adjuster(s) must first examine the site for damage and report this to the coordinator of disaster recovery and his company. He then permits the team to visit the site and begin the recovery effort.

3.8 Recovery Team Examines the Site

The recovery team will make an initial examination of the damage at the primary site and make a decision as to which manufacturers and suppliers to call in to make a more detailed examination and submit a problem report to them.

3.9 Manufacturers' Representatives Examine Primary Site

All manufacturers' representatives (customer engineers) will examine their equipment and report back to the team the extent of the damage, the need to repair/replace, and the estimated time for repair/replacement.

3.10 Presentation of Outage Report to Recovery Team

The manufacturers' representatives will present a comprehensive report (see Outage Form) of their findings to the recovery team and data processing committee. This report is used by the committees to decide whether to go off-site for processing or delay processing until the primary site is restored.

3.11 Recovery Team Makes an Inventory
of Missing/Damaged Items

The recovery team makes a list of all the missing or damaged items to be used in recovering the primary site or processing at the recovery site.

3.12 Data Processing Committee Decides on Behalf
of the Primary Site or Recovery Site

The data processing committee will use the outage problem report to determine whether to process at the recovery site or delay processing until the primary site is restored. The committee will then notify the recovery team of this decision.

3.13 Notify Recovery Site of Disaster

The head of the data processing committee or his delegate will notify the appropriate members at the recovery site of the disaster at HealthWays and the need to process at that site. The notification will be given first by phone and then by a letter.

The following personnel will be notified:

		Telephone	
Name	Company	Home	Office
Recovery Center	Comdisco		896-9500
Ed Lawn	Comdisco		896-9500

3.14 Order Vital Supplies

The recovery team will indicate to the various people responsible for ordering supplies the vital items that are stored off-site that must be ordered and delivered to the recovery site.

3.15 Retrieve Vital Items from Off-site Storage

The recovery team will indicate to the various people responsible for ordering supplies the vital items that are stored off-site that must be retrieved and taken to the recovery site.

3.16 Prepare Recovery Site

The members of the recovery team responsible for preparing the recovery site will prepare the environment for office staff (if necessary), data entry operators (if necessary), and the operations and programming staff.

3.17 Coordinate Movement of Staff to Recovery Site

The recovery team will coordinate the movement of staff to the Comdisco disaster recovery site. The team will also coordinate the transportation needs of the staff.

3.18 Notify Staff of Alternate Duties

The recovery team, acting on the advice of the various department heads, will notify HealthWays staff of alternate duties that they will perform during the disaster period.

3.19 Suspend All Application Program Development and Maintenance

The recovery team will instruct the MIS department and the users to suspend all development of existing and new programs and the maintenance of all programs.

3.20 Move Needed Supplies to Recovery Site

The recovery team will coordinate the movement of all necessary supplies to the Comdisco disaster recovery site.

3.21 Load Operating System at Recovery Site

The systems/programmer and operations staff will off-load the operating system tape and test the system to ensure that it can support the production requirements during the disaster period.

3.22 Load Production Programs and Data Files and Hook Up Terminals

The systems/programmer and operations staff will off-load the production programs and data files. The online and batch production programs should then be tested to ensure that the production requirements can be met during the disaster period.

3.23 Run Scheduled Production Jobs at Recovery Site

The operations staff will run scheduled production jobs at the recovery site. The recovery team will monitor the data processing needs of the users during the disaster period and make adjustments to the production schedule as necessary.

4.0 Disaster Recovery Action Plan (Primary Site Restoration)

4.1 Introduction

This section describes the actions that will be taken by HealthWays to restore the primary site and commence normal production processing.

The section continues the action plan from the previous section where a decision is made to restore the primary site.

4.2 Notify Staff of Alternate Duties

The recovery team acting on the advice of the various department heads will notify HealthWays staff of alternate duties that they will perform during the disaster period.

4.3 Conduct a General Cleanup and Salvage at Primary Site

The recovery team will coordinate the conduct of a general cleanup and salvage of items at the primary site.

4.4 Order Vital Supplies

The recovery team will indicate to the various people responsible for ordering supplies the vital items that must be ordered and delivered to the primary site.

4.5 Secure the Primary Site

The recovery team will study the physical security needs of the primary site and add security as is necessary to secure the site during the disaster period.

4.6 Start General Report and Replacement of Computer Room and Environment

The recovery team will coordinate the general repair/replacement of the computer room and computer environment.

4.7 Start General Repair and Replacement of Computer and Peripherals

The recovery team will coordinate the general repair/replacement of the computer and all required peripherals.

4.8 Retrieve Vital Items from Off-site Storage

The recovery team will coordinate the retrieval of vital items from the off-site storage facilities and move them to the primary site.

4.9 Load the Operating System

The systems/programming and operations staff will load the operating system and run a test to ensure that it is operable.

4.10 Connect and Start Up Online System

The systems/programming and operations staff will load the online programs and test the system to ensure that it is operable.

4.11 Start Up and Test Batch Programs

The systems/programming, applications, and operations staff will load the batch programs and test them to ensure that they are operable.

5.0 Activity Areas and Departments

5.1 Introduction

This section describes the breakdown of HealthWays into various activity areas of departments for the purpose of effecting the disaster recovery plan and meeting the stated objectives of the plan.

The activity areas are better defined as areas in which certain disaster recovery-related activities are conducted to effect the recovery of the primary site and data processing at the recovery site.

5.2 List of Activity Areas

The activity areas are made up of the following:

• MIS Management/Department
• Systems Programming
• Application Programming
• Production Scheduler and Operations
• User Departments

a. Claims
b. Billing and Enrollment
c. Accounting/Finance
d. Health Services
e. Marketing

- Equipment Manufacturers
- Transportation
- Recovery Team
- Data Processing Committee

6.0 List of Activities by Activity Area

6.1 Introduction

This section describes the activities conducted in the various activity areas. The activities were compiled during the responses from the various questionnaires and research material on disaster recovery planning.

6.2 MIS Activity List

The following activities will be carried out by MIS in the event of a disaster:

1. Coordinate restoration effort at the primary site.
2. Coordinate production processing at recovery site.
3. Coordinate retrieval from various off-site storage locations of vital items and deliver to recovery site.
4. Schedule the processing of production jobs based on priority established by the recovery team, the data processing committee, and user departments.
5. Coordinate the circulation of tapes and off-site storage of backup files.
6. Monitor the backup and recovery procedures during the disaster period.
7. Monitor the online processing service level and the response time during the disaster period.
8. Offer technical support to various user departments during the disaster period.

6.3 System Application Programming Activity List

The following activities will be carried out by the systems and application programming groups during the disaster period:

1. Load and test the operating system and production programs during the disaster period.
2. Assist in running scheduled production jobs.
3. Assist in backing up critical files.
4. Assist in restoring critical software at the primary site.
5. Assist in the maintenance of DOS/VSE, ICCF, CICS, and utility programs during the disaster period.

6.4 Production Scheduler and Operations

The production scheduler and operations group will be responsible for the following activities:

1. Schedule and run critical programs as indicated by the recovery team.
2. Coordinate the intermediate storage of critical reports.
3. Coordinate the transportation and distribution of critical reports.
4. Assist in the off-site storage of critical files.

6.5 User Department Activity List

The activities of the various user departments that contribute to the recovery of data processing services at HealthWays are listed in Sections 10.3 and 10.4. The readers are referred to these sections for further information.

6.6 Equipment Manufacturers Activity List

The various equipment manufacturers will examine the damage done to equipment at the primary site and report the extent of the damage to the recovery team. The manufacturers are required to fill out the "Outage Due to Disasters Reporting" form and return it to the team. A copy of the form can be found in Section 18.

6.7 Coordination of Transportation Activity List

The transportation needs of the various user departments were obtained by surveys and listed in Appendix B. The coordinator of transportation will ensure that those needs are met during a disaster.

6.8 Recovery Team Activity List

The recovery team activity list was given in Section 2. The readers are referred to this section for further information.

6.9 Data Processing Committee Activity List

The functions of the data processing committee were outlined in the administrative procedures manual. Readers are referred to this manual for further information.

7.0 Disaster Notification List

7.1 Introduction

The analyst who writes the disaster plan would, at this point, list all the personnel within and outside the organization who should be notified of a disaster. The compiled list should be generated by department within the organization.

8.0 Disaster Recovery Activities — Primary Site

8.1 Introduction

This section describes the various activities that must be carried out at the primary site to restore it to a predisaster state.
  The activities at the primary site fall into the following categories:

* Disaster declaration
* Disaster notification
* Assessment of damages
* Vital items retrieval

- Site cleanup
- Physical security maintenance
- Repair/replacement equipment and computer room
- Load and test operation system
- Load and test application program
- Back up vital items
- Back up and restore input transactions
- Replace missing documentation and procedure manuals.

8.2 Disaster Declaration

The data processing committee and the recovery team will declare that a disaster has occurred at HealthWays. The coordinator of the recovery team will in turn ask the coordinator of disaster notification to notify all relevant personnel on the disaster notification list of the declaration.

8.3 Disaster Notification

The coordinator of Disaster notification will notify all personnel on the list of the occurrence of the disaster.

8.4 Retrieval of Vital Items

The recovery team will retrieve from all off-site storage locations vital items that are necessary to the restoration of the primary site.
   The vital items and their off-site storage locations are listed in Section 16.0.

8.5 Primary Site Cleanup

The recovery team will coordinate the cleanup of the primary site and assign various staff members to alternate duties in this regard.

8.6 Physical Security Maintenance

The recovery team will ensure that adequate physical security is maintained at all times during the restoration of the primary site.

8.7 Repair/Replace Computer Room and Equipment

The various equipment manufacturers will coordinate their efforts and resources to repair/replace the computer room and equipment.

The member of the recovery team who has been assigned to coordinate the rebuilding of the primary site will monitor the progress and report on a regular basis to the team and the data processing committee.

8.8 Load and Test Operating System

The systems/programmer and operations staff will be responsible for loading and testing the operating system at the primary site.

8.9 Primary Site Recovery Checklist

The following items should be checked after recovery at the primary site:

1. Make sure all libraries are installed.
2. Make sure system IPLs normally.
3. Make sure VTAM starts up error-free and all terminals, PU, and lines are activated.
4. Make sure CICS comes up successfully. There should be no errors for any of the resources defined in CICS control tables.
5. Log on to CICS, ICCF, and BVSM to do inquiry or updates.
6. Try a small batch job.

9.0 Disaster Recovery Activities — Recovery Site

9.1 Introduction

This section describes the various activities that must be carried out at the recovery site to allow HealthWays to continue to process data at an acceptable level during the disaster period.

The activities at the recovery site fall into the following categories:

• Prepare recovery site and ready area offices
• Load operating system and NCP Gen

- Deliver vital items and supplies from off-site storage and other suppliers
- Load application package and data files
- Make necessary changes to operating system and software
- Conduct minimal testing of operating system and software
- Run prioritized production jobs
- Wrap up activities and removal to restored primary site

9.2 Prepare Recovery Site and Ready Area Offices

The first activity to be conducted at the recovery site is the preparation of the site and ready area.

The site preparation will include:

- Initial system generation
- Initial test of online and batch programs
- Review test results with Comdisco
- Retest online and batch as necessary
- Notify Comdisco that a disaster has occurred
- Move office furniture and terminals into ready area
- Test online transactions from ready area
- Install telephone equipment and other office equipment as required
- Initiate delivery and distribution system for ready area

9.3 Run Prioritized Production Jobs

The recovery team in conjunction with the users and data processing committee will schedule jobs to be processed at the recovery site base on the criticality of the jobs.

The criticality and hence the priority of the jobs will be based on the greatest contribution made by that job to the survival of the corporation.

The contribution may be in terms of finances or support to the largest number of users within the corporation.

In addition to the criteria listed above, the priority given to a job may be based on the length of time required for processing and the competition for resources among jobs.

9.4 Wrap-Up Activities and Process at Primary Site

The operations staff will conduct wrap-up activities at Comdisco upon termination of processing there. The wrap-up activities will include:

- Review of service level obtained during disaster
- Review of transportation needs
- Review of report distribution procedures
- Review of environment suitability and security
- Review of online performance and response time
- Review of existing contingency procedures
- Review of recovery procedures
- Remove all disaster recovery items to primary site
- Make changes to plan wherever necessary

9.4.1 Review of Service Level

The recovery team and the data processing committee will review the level of service that was provided to the users during the disaster period.

The level of service provided during the disaster can be measured as follows:

- Response time for online processing
- Number or percent of total terminals supported during the disaster
- Turn-around time for batch reports
- Time to resolve problems
- Effective and efficient resolution of problems

The recovery team and the data processing committee will evaluate the level of service provided during the disaster period and make recommendations that will improve the level of service.

9.4.2 Review of Transportation Needs

The recovery team will review the actual transportation needs against the predicted needs and make recommendations to improve the transportation that was provided.

9.4.3 Review of Environment Suitability and Security

The recovery team and the data processing committee will review the recovery site environment for suitability and security.

The areas that must be reviewed are the ready area and the areas for holding reports before they are distributed.

The team and committee will decide on a set of measurements by which the environment can be evaluated. These measurements may include:

- Functionality
- Security
- Transportation and parking
- Secure holding areas
- Ease of access to facilities

10.0 Vital Areas Recovery

10.1 Introduction

In this section of the plan, the analyst should list the vital records that MIS must have in a ready status in order to recover from a disaster. It also should list the vital functions, procedures, and reports that must be preserved in each department to assist in the recovery of the primary site and accomplish processing at the recovery site.

The section should also detail any contracted for reports or legal filings that MIS must assist the relevant departments in producing during the disaster period to meet their obligations.

Finally, the section should list the vital areas in MIS that must be preserved to assist in the recovery from a disaster.

10.2 List of Vital Records and Files

The analyst should prepare a list of vital records and files with the following format:

Department	Vital Records
Accounting	General Ledger
Health Services	Utilization Review

10.3 User Departments Vital Functions

Department	Vital Functions
Accounting	1. Restoration of general ledger
	2. Restoration of historical files with respect to the physician association risk pools
Health Services	1. Utilization review
	2. Ancillary services referrals
	3. Review case to determine degree of emergency
Billing/Enrollment	1. Receive and batch source documents
	2. Capture revenue-related information for accounting purposes
Claims	1. Reprocess lost entered or adjudicated claims
	2. Request physicians to resubmit lost claims
Member Services	1. Maintain contact with members
	2. Mail membership kit
	3. Document changes to physician address and phone number
	4. Screen member submitted bills

10.4 User Departments Recovery Functions

Department	Recovery Functions
Claims	1. Reprocess lost claims
	2. Request resubmittals from providers
	3. Reinput lost physician files
	4. Enter new physician or provider information
	5. Process existing original claims

Department	Recovery Functions
Member Services	1. Forward membership change forms
	2. Forward conversion applications
	3. Forward member-submitted bills

10.5 MIS Vital Transactions Recovery Procedures

All transactions that are not backed up before a disaster strikes will be reconstructed through the use of available source documents. Each functional area will be maintaining a file (manual) of the last two days of processing.

In the event a disaster destroys the in-house tape library, the off-site copy will be recalled. This copy will be restored, hence data will be restored to a two-days prior copy. The two-day file of source documents will then be used to update the data base to a current status. If the source documents are destroyed, the updates to the database could only be made if a second request is eventually presented to HealthWays by the member or employer.

10.6 MIS Retrieval from Off-Site Storage Procedures

MIS currently maintains two off-site storage locations. They are:

1. HealthWays Systems, Inc. — North Office
2. Iron Mountain

10.6.1 Recovery Procedures for North Office

Items stored:	Forms, supplies, checks
Location:	50 Tice Boulevard
	Woodcliff Lake, NJ 07675
Telephone:	(201) 930-4999

Disaster Recovery Procedures: Call Office Manager, (914) 496-5761, who will meet personnel at the office and allow retrieval of items.

10.6.2 Recovery Procedures for Iron Mountain

Items stored: See off-site storage list
Location: Iron Mountain Group, Inc.
    P.O. Box 86
    Rosendale, NY 12472
Telephone: (914) 658-3132

Disaster Recovery Procedures: Call Iron Mountain Group, Inc. (914) 658-3132, wait for someone to answer. Give them your name, company name, tape serial number needed, documentation box numbers needed, and the telephone number that data site personnel can call back in order to confirm the request. Data site personnel will call back 20 to 40 minutes later, verify information, verify individual has authority to request tapes (e.g., individual is on the signature card).

Data site personnel should also confirm where tapes should be sent. If tapes are to be sent to the recovery site (Comdisco), you must inform them, as well as give them directions to the site.

Personnel who call the off-site storage location must know the password and be prepared to authenticate the password.

The retrieval process from first phone call until tapes are selected from vault and loaded into van should take about 40 minutes.

11.0 Equipment Inventory

11.1 Introduction

The Analyst should prepare a list of all the equipment currently owned by the organization. This list should include the name of the department that owns the equipment, the model number of the equipment, and the vendor of the equipment.

The format of the list is as follows:

Equipment	Model No	Vendor	Owner Department
Mainframe Computer	3090-B	IBM	Accounting

12.0 Telecommunications Requirement

12.1 Introduction

This section discusses the telecommunication requirements that will satisfy HealthWays online needs during a disaster. The requirements are as follows:

- Modify VTAM books defining the terminals and printers required at the recovery site.
- Modify VTAM books for remote terminals to incorporate various macros used by NCP.
- Catalog above books in source statement library.
- Include above books in startup books for VTAM.
- Linkedit the assembled NCP Gen from Comdisco with the name specified in build macro of NCP Gen and catalog it into core image library.

13.0 Sites Security

13.1 Introduction

This section discusses physical security at the primary and recovery sites. The data in this section must be kept current for auditing and insurance purposes. Some recommendations for a data security study are also included.

13.2 Physical Security at Primary Site

The existing physical security at the primary site is currently negligible. This section will be updated as more physical security mechanisms are installed.

13.3 Physical Security at the Recovery Site

The existing physical security at the recovery site is described in the recovery support manuals obtainable from Comdisco. The security is currently more than adequate for our existing needs, and therefore we do not expect to make any further demands on them for enhanced security.

13.4 Data Security Study for Primary Site

As HealthWays' data processing environment grows, there will be increased opportunities for breaches of security. The disaster recovery plan recommends that data security studies be conducted from time to time. The studies will encompass the following areas:

* Review threats to which the corporation is exposed
* Review available protection mechanisms to counter the threats
* Categorize the threats into:

  a. Accidental
  b. Deliberate

* Categorize protection mechanisms into:

  a. External — Outside the operating system
  b. Internal — Residing in the operating system

* Evaluate adequacy of protection mechanisms
* Evaluate likelihood of reoccurrence of specific threats
* Recommend protection mechanisms in light of disaster findings

14.0 Disaster Recovery Plan Testing

14.1 Introduction

Testing of the disaster recovery plan is necessary to ensure that:

* The plan is complete and workable
* The materials and data are available and usable to perform alternate processing for critical applications
* The system and library files, application software, and production date files can be restored when normal processing is resumed

   The testing of the plan described in this section encompasses three separate levels of testing, with each level incorporating more complex and comprehensive lower levels.
   The three levels are:

Level I   — Adequacy of off-site storage of files and documentation
Level II — Restoration of the primary site using off-site files and documentation
Level III — System restoration on the recovery site computer

Every time a test is performed, a brief report must be prepared, with copies furnished to the following:

• Vice President — MIS
• Manager — MIS

14.1.1 Areas to Be Tested

• Backup for

 — VSAM files
 — Tesseract Programs
 — JCL
 — Operating System
• Documentation Backup for

 — Operations
 — Operating System
 — Tesseract Programs
• Recovery Procedures

 — System Recovery
 — Data file
• Supplies Backup

14.1.2 Types of Tests to Be Conducted

• Dependent on Scope of Test

 — One aspect
 — Several related aspects
 — Full-scale test
• Dependent on Test Mode

 — Actual processing test
• Phased Approach

 — Test contents of off-site storage
 — Recover critical system using off-site data at primary site
 — Recover critical system using off-site data at recovery site

14.1.3 Steps in Conducting Test

- Select subjects of test
- Determine objectives of test
- Collect test results during and after test
- Evaluate results
- Report successes, failures, and resolution to problems
- Modify disaster plan accordingly

14.1.4 Specific Parts of Plan That Can Be Tested

- Ability to retrieve documents from off-site storage
- Recovery of one or more critical systems using data stored off-site
- Ability to recover operating system at primary site from files stored off-site
- Ability to recover operating system at recovery site
- Availability of support equipment
- Availability of peripheral equipment
- Ability to activate plan in disaster
- Availability of supplies
- Availability of special forms and supplies
- Security measures and security bypass procedures

14.2 Level I Testing

Level I testing of the disaster recovery plan is concerned with the adequacy of off-site storage of files and documentation and ability to retrieve same. Level I testing should be performed at least twice a year. The testing consists of the following:

1. Select applications to be tested
2. Availability of data and documentation; e.g., can available information be used to locate and identify the necessary backup files?
3. Document the disaster simulation assumptions and events:
   a. Recovery assignments and responsibilities
   b. Factors necessary for efficient recovery
   c. Information required prior to the test
4. Obtain a list of all production files and programs

5. Proceed with recovery of selected applications, identifying problems such as:

    a. Missing or incomplete files
    b. Missing or incomplete documentation
    c. Operational problems
    d. Availability of user-maintained data such as current transactions and source documents

14.3 Level II Testing

Level II testing of the disaster recovery plan is concerned with system restoration at the primary site using off-site files and documentation. Level II testing should be performed at least once per year. The testing consists of the five procedures listed above and a sixth procedure — to evaluate the effectiveness of the overall plan, analyze problems, and make changes where necessary.

14.4 Level III Testing

Level III testing of the disaster recovery plan is concerned with system restoration at the recovery site with a reduced staff. Level III testing should be performed at least once per year. The testing consists of the six procedures listed above — Level II testing plus a seventh step — to proceed with restoration of system residence and library files, noting the approximate elapsed time required.

14.5 Simulated Disaster and Fire Drill

At least once per year, MIS should conduct a test of the disaster recovery plan which will include simulating a disaster and conducting a "fire drill." The test may be as simple as having the coordinator of the recovery team request that the computer system be brought down, without prior notice, and restored from tapes and files stored off-site. The "fire drill" will then require that one goes through the retrieval procedures and have the vital items delivered to the primary site within a reasonable period.

The recovery team may want to involve the user departments in the "fire drill" and have them support the restoration of DP services by reentering "lost" transactions.

15.0 Disaster Recovery Plan Maintenance

15.1 Introduction

The disaster recovery plan will be verified to be current semiannually by the appropriate functional staff under the direction of the manager-MIS. Evidence of the verification will be reported in writing to the vice president-MIS.

Particular emphasis should be given to keeping the appendices current as soon as a change in status becomes known, and should be reflected by immediate issuance of revised pages. (Examples: telephone number, personnel, priority of applications, transportation needs, and off-site storage items.)

A review schedule should be established to assure correctness of the computer hardware configuration section and its compatibility with hardware at the recovery site.

Revisions to the appropriate plan sections will be made as required, and revised pages will be issued to the holders of the plan.

15.2 Maintenance of the Disaster Recovery Plan

The disaster recovery plan should be updated by the coordinator of the recovery team and all holders of the plan.

15.3 How to Keep the Plan Current

A cover memorandum giving instructions for inserting and removing documents from your manual will be sent with each manual revision. For each revision, do the following:

• Read the memo carefully
• Remove obsolete or superseded documents, if directed to do so
• Place revisions in the manual in the proper order
• File the cover memo behind the last section in the manual so that you have a record of all revisions that you receive

15.4 Initiating Revisions

Notify the coordinator of the disaster recovery team when you become aware that a change — addition, deletion, or revision — to the content of the plan is necessary.

Responsibilities for Plan Maintenance List

Section No. Frequency	Section Name	Responsibility	Frequency
	Plan Distribution	Coordinator	A
	Names, Telephone nos.	Notifications Coordinator	Q
	Recovery Site Backup	Coordinator	A
	Materials Checklist	Notifications Coordinator	Q
	Off-site Storage	Manager-MIS	Q
	Location and Contents Vendor Directory	Manager-MIS	Q
	Application Inventory	Applications	Q
	Hardware Inventory	Operators	Q
	Software Inventory	Systems Programmer	Q
	Documentation Inventory	Applications	Q
	Application Priority	Recovery Team	Q
	Disaster Recovery Plan Maintenance	Coordinator	Q

A=Annually
Q=Quarterly

15.5 Monitoring Performance of the Disaster Recovery Plan

The following items should serve as a checklist for monitoring the performance of the disaster recovery plan:

1. Generate an operating system at the primary or recovery site from files stored off-site
2. Retrieve items from off-site storage
3. Test online and batch programs
4. Test north/south office to Comdisco remote processing
5. Ability to update hardware and software
6. Ability to update any listed item in plan; e.g., critical employees or phone numbers
7. Ability to monitor changes semiannually
8. Documentation backup
9. Backup to critical people
10. Modify disaster plan according to test results
11. Availability of peripheral and support equipment
12. Availability of forms and supplies
13. Monitor implementable security features
14. Test for missing or incomplete files
15. Test for missing or incomplete documentation
16. Test ability to restore system resident and library files

16.0 Off-Site Storage Requirements

16.1 Introduction

This section discusses the items that HealthWays must store off-site and be able to retrieve within a 24-hour period to assist them in the restoration of the primary site and continued processing at the recovery site.

It also indicates the storage requirements of various user departments. The lists are given by departments and show the location of the off-site storage facility.

Department	Off-Site Location	Item
MIS	Iron Mountain Group	ICCF
	P.O. Box 86	System File
	Rosendale, NY 12472	Tesseract Program
	Phone: (914) 658-3132	CPS
		BPA
		Fast Copy of 220 to 227
		Tesseract Documentation
		MIS Operator's Manual
		MIS Contingency Plan
		MIS Administrative Manual

Department	Off-Site Location	Item
Claims	Access Self Storage 135 Amboy Avenue Woodbridge, NJ 07095 Phone: 750-1440	Claims Remittance Advices
	Abrams Residence 37 Dobson Road Edison, NJ 08817	1974 CRV ICD-9 Text Medicare Policy Manual Training Manual Policy & Procedure Manual Current Provider Listing
Health Services	HealthWays North Office 50 Tice Boulevard Woodcliff Lake, NJ Phone: 930-4999	Original Provider Contracts
	Apperson Business Forms	Admission Certifications Claim Forms

17.0 Preventive Measures

17.1 Introduction

This section discusses some preventive measures that HealthWays can implement to either prevent a disaster or minimizing the impact of a disaster.

The reader should be cognizant of the fact that a disaster may result from causes such as, fire, flood, electrical storms, or sabotage by disgruntled employees. Disaster may also occur if equipment is not maintained as specified and problems due to component failures are ignored.

The preventive measures discussed below will include:

• Component failure analysis
• Conducting risk assessments
• Installing protection mechanisms
• System outage analysis

The section ends with some recommendations for disaster prevention and physical and data security.

17.2 Component Failure Analysis (CFA)

Component failure analysis is a technique designed to raise the level of system availability by finding ways to shorten recovery times when a system component fails. It is a systematic approach to help management predict and evaluate the impact of a component failure on those applications thought to be most critical to the organization, assess current backup and recovery capability, and consider alternatives designed to improve availability.

MIS management should keep statistics on the various peripheral devices regarding frequency of outage, type of outage, applications affected, cost and type of backup available, and availability of replacement.

These statistics can be used to predict future performance of equipment, select equipment, and assist MIS staff in responding to various component failures and minimize the impact of these failures.

17.3 Conducting Risk Assessments

MIS should conduct risk assessment studies to determine the likelihood of a specific threat occurring, the loss to the corporation if this threat occurred, and the protection mechanism needed to counter the threat. The results from the risk assessment study can be used to prevent a threat from occurring, minimize the impact if a specific threat occurred, and install protection mechanisms to counter specific threats.

17.4 Install Protection Mechanisms

MIS should install mechanisms that will ensure both physical and data security in the computer environment.

In the area of physical security, MIS should control access to the computer environment by requiring the use of badges or number combination locks. They should also consider the use of fire prevention or abatement equipment in the computer room.

In the area of data security, MIS should control access to the stored data by requiring universal use of passwords; more control over the use, distribution, and storage of passwords; and the installation of control mechanisms such as authorization tables, access control facility (ACF), resource access control facility (RACF), and GUARDIAN.

17.5 System Outage Analysis (SOA)

Like component failure analysis, the objective of system outage analysis is to raise the level of system availability by finding ways to shorten recovery times when a system fails. Unlike component failure analysis, the objects dealt with in SOA are programs and not hardware. MIS can gather statistics on applications failure, existing backup, and restore program failures, and read/write errors. These statistics can be used to minimize the impact of these failures and increase the efficiency of the applications.

18.0 Disaster Recovery Forms

The next several pages illustrate the forms that can be used to collect recovery data.

HEALTHWAYS SYSTEMS, INC.
EQUIPMENT INVENTORY FORM
(DISASTER RECOVERY)

DEPARTMENT: _____   FORM NO.: _____

                                DATE: _____

Equipment Name   Model No.   Manufacturer

HEALTHWAYS SYSTEMS, INC.
RECOVERY PLAN DISTRIBUTION LIST
(DISASTER RECOVERY)

FORM NO.: _____

DATE: _____

Person Name   Department/Address   Number of Copies

HEALTHWAYS SYSTEMS, INC.
OFF-SITE STORAGE LIST
(DISASTER RECOVERY)

DEPARTMENT: _____   FORM NO.: _____

DATE: _____

Item Name	Used By	Location of Storage	Phone	
			Business	Nonbusiness

HEALTHWAYS SYSTEMS, INC.
SUPPLIERS NOTIFICATION FORM
(DISASTER RECOVERY)

DEPARTMENT: _____   FORM NO.: _____

DATE: _____

			Phone	
Supplier	Salesman	Supplies	Home	Office

HEALTHWAYS SYSTEMS, INC.
DISASTER NOTIFICATION FORM
(DISASTER RECOVERY)

DEPARTMENT: _____   FORM NO.: _____

DATE: _____

Name	Company	Recovery Responsibility	Phone	
			Home	Office

HEALTHWAYS SYSTEMS, INC.
PROBLEM REPORTING FORM
(DISASTER RECOVERY)

FORM NO.: _____

DATE: _____

OUTAGES DUE TO DISASTERS REPORTING FORM

Analysis of Outage Section:

_____

Problem-Reporting Section:

_____

Component Damage-Reporting Section:
Component
   Name   Model No.   Description of Damage

_____

Manufacturers Notification Section:
                         Notification
Manufacturer   Equipment   Person/Time

_____

Recovery Time Estimate Section:
Component
   Name   Model No.   Estimated Date/Time

_____

Recommendation Section:

B

Processing Alternatives
Available to HealthWays

1.1 Introduction

The following appendix describes the processing scenarios available to HealthWays during a disaster. They are as follows:

1. Process at Comdisco with north and south offices
2. Process at Comdisco with remote terminals from the north office
3. Process at Comdisco with remote terminals from the south office
4. Process at Comdisco with ready area used as offices

1.2 Process at Comdisco with North and South Offices

HealthWays will make a decision, in the event of a disaster, to process at the recovery site with remote processing from the north and south offices.

The decision will be based on the following:

1. Transportation needs
2. Office space requirements

3. Limitations on number of terminals
4. Cost
5. Staff requirement
6. Supervision requirement
7. Technical support
8. Communication needs
9. Response time consideration

1.2.1 Transportation Needs

The transportation needs will reflect the requirements to move personnel, data and reports and vital documents or supplies to Comdisco, north and south offices.

The survey has indicated that the company van will be heavily utilized in transporting the above-mentioned items. These requirements must be matched against alternatives in order to determine the recovery processing environment.

1.2.2 Office Space Requirements

The minimum office space requirement to relocate critical employees from the central office to either Comdisco, the north or south office was established by the responses to the user department survey on disaster recovery. The requirements are listed in Appendix B.

1.2.3 Limitations of the Number of Terminals

The minimum number of terminals needed by the user areas and MIS was determined from the surveys to be 22. The controllers at both the north and south offices can be expanded to accommodate 32 terminals each. As the corporation grows, the minimum number of terminals will change. The survey indicates that remote processing can be fully supported (from the telecommunications aspect) at any of the satellite offices.

1.2.4 Cost

The analyst will determine several cost alternatives and present them to the executives for their consideration.

1.2.5 Staff Requirement

The minimum number of critical employees required to support HealthWays during a disaster period was set at 43 by surveys. These 43 people plus executives, the recovery team, and a few support staff will require space at the north and south offices if the recovery team decided that that was the best processing environment to use in order to enable HealthWays to recover from a disaster.

1.2.6 Staff Supervision Requirement

The requirement to supervise staff at two locations is a factor that must be taken into consideration when deciding on the processing environment for HealthWays during the disaster period.

This becomes even more critical if one supervisor has to look after the day-to-day operations of staff at both locations or because of reduced staff senior management has to supervise staff in the two locations.

1.2.7 Technical Support

HealthWays must take into account the ability of a reduced technical support staff to respond to user problems at two offices during the disaster period.

The MIS technical staff will be required to support the data processing effort at the recovery site and the restoration effort at the primary site.

The technical staff will also be required to assist in resolution of problems in the online and telecommunications network during the disaster period. A decision to operate two offices during this period will take this factor into consideration.

1.2.8 Communication Needs

HealthWays must determine the communication needs of the two offices when making a decision to process at Comdisco with the north and south offices as remote nodes.

The communication needs will include voice communication and online communication for terminals at both offices.

During a disaster, normal communication flow may be disrupted. Employees may be working under stressful conditions and tend to bypass procedures.

HealthWays should also consider how messages are transferred between offices and the recovery site and the need to protect the information flow between offices.

1.2.9 Response Time Consideration

HealthWays must consider the online processing response time when processing from Comdisco and using the north and south offices as remote nodes (locations).

The response time will suffer some degradation, especially if dial-up facilities are used to communicate with Comdisco.

1.3 Process at Comdisco with North Office

HealthWays has the option of processing data at Comdisco with the north office as a remote node.

The decision to process in this environment will be based on the same nine criteria discussed in Section 1.2 of this chapter. In addition to the above criteria, HealthWays should also consider the following advantages:

1. All critical staff in same location
2. Functional departments in close proximity to each other
3. Logistics of moving personnel and equipment is simplified
4. Technical support can be concentrated in same location

1.4 Process at Comdisco with South Office

HealthWays has the option of processing data at Comdisco with the south office as a remote node.

The decision to process in this environment will be based on the same nine criteria discussed in Section 1.2 of this chapter. In addition to the above criteria, HealthWays should also consider the following advantages:

1. All critical staff in same location
2. Functional departments in close proximity to each other

3. Logistics of moving personnel and equipment is simplified
4. Technical support can be concentrated in same location

1.5 Process at Comdisco with Ready Area at Comdisco Used As Offices

HealthWays has the option of processing data at Comdisco and using the ready area there as offices.

The same nine criteria used in Section 1.2 can be used to make this processing decision. However, the advantages and disadvantages of processing in this environment should also be considered. Following are some advantages:

1. Proximity to reduced technical staff
2. Minimum disruption to north and south offices
3. Transportation and communication needs to one central office
4. Ready area with space to accommodate 100+ desks and filing cabinets
5. Ready area with built-in facilities for dial-up communication with mainframe

C

Transportation Needs

The following is a list by department of the transportation needs:

Department	Transportation Needs
Member Services	Personal transportation
Health Services	Company van to move data, reports, and vital items
Claims	Company van to transport management, supervisors, and key examiners plus listings, department logs, training manuals, and claims
Accounting	Company van to move personnel data, reports, and vital documents

2.0 Reports Distribution Plan

The analyst must determine whom within the organization should receive reports during the disaster. The distribution plan may have a simple format as follows:

Personnel	*Report*	*Delivery Method*
President	Progress Report on Disaster	Hand Delivered

3.0 Office Space Requirements

The following is the office space requirement for each department as determined by surveys:

Department	Office Space Requirements
Member Services	500 sq. ft. or 15 desks, 4 filing cabinets
Health Services	7 desks, 1 filing cabinet
Claims	Long term: (a) one shift: 9 desks, filing cabinet, work table (b) two shifts: 5 desks, filing cabinet, work table Short term: (a) one shift: 10 desks, filing cabinet (b) two shifts: 5 desks, filing cabinet
Accounting	300 square feet or 10 desks
Billing/Enrollment	4 desks, filing cabinets
MIS	4 desks and filing cabinets
Marketing	7 desks, 1 filing cabinet

Note: 1 desk requires 36 sq. ft.

4.0 Schedule of Jobs by Priorities

The analyst will determine the schedule for running production jobs during the disaster. This schedule must be worked out with the aid of the Data Recovery Committee and the Recovery Team.

D

Disaster Plan Distribution List

The following is the list of personnel by department who will receive copies of the Disaster Recovery Plan:

Person Name	Department/Address	Number of Copies
Pat Akellian	V.P. Mktg. & Admin.	1
Cindy Hoefsmit	Marketing Manager	1
Lynette Carter	Asst. Mgr., Member Services	10
Eleanore Matthiesen	Sr. Rep., Member Services	1
Kathy Fluhr	Sr. Rep., Member Services	1
Betty Kimmel	V.P. Health Services	1
Cindy Mazer	Health Services	1
Joann Vint	Health Services	1
Vice Pres.-Finance	Claims	1
Controller	Finance	1
Manager	Claims	1

Person Name	Department/Address	Number of Copies
Asst. Manager	Claims	1
Shailesh Asher	Accounting	1
Thomas Hartnett	HealthWays Systems	1
Joseph Papa	HealthWays Inc.	1
Charles Miller	Billing	1
Arline Connor	Billing	1

2.0 List of Critical Reports

The following is a list of critical reports by departments:

Department	Critical Reports
Health Services	1. Weekly inpatient utilization 2. Monthly inpatient utilization 3. Outstanding inpatient bills
Claims	1. Pending claims report 2. Claims entered and adjudicated 3. Provider listing 4. Eligibility listing
Accounting	1. Lag reports 2. Membership reports
Billing/Enrollment	1. Group and individual bills 2. Group billing register

3.0 Priority of Critical Programs

The following is a list of critical programs by priority within department:

Department	Critical Programs
Member Services	1. Active member eligibility report 2. Terminated employee report 3. Dependent age cut-off report 4. Aged pending claims
Health Services	1. Monthly inpatient utilization report 2. Outstanding inpatient bills 3. Weekly inpatient utilization report
Claims	1. Adjudicated but not paid claims 2. Entered but not adjudicated claims
Accounting	1. Lag reports 2. Membership reports
Billing/Enrollment	1. Group bills 2. Individual bills 3. Group billing register

4.0 Critical Employees

The following is a list of critical employees by department who are vital to the survival of HealthWays during a disaster:

Department	Critical Employees
Member Services	All reps and clerk typists
Health Services	Betty Kimmel Cindy Mazer Joann Vint
Claims (See attached list)	Manager Assistant Manager Supervisors Claims Examiners
Accounting	Don Picuri Shailesh Asher
Billing/Enrollment	Charles Miller Arline Connor

Department	Critical Employees
MIS	Jay Ruparel
	Simon Baskerville
	Denis Roy
Marketing	

E

Critical Supplies List

The following is a list of critical supplies by departments within HealthWays:

Department	Critical Supplies List
Member Services	Membership Change Form Transmittal Forms Reimbursement Forms Membership Kits Physician Directors Group and Individual Membership Service Agreements
Health Services	Computer Terminals Hospital Logs Member Applications Admission Certification Forms Claim Forms
Claims	No. 10 Safety Window Envelopes Commercial Copying 74 CRV Medical Policy Manual Additional Info & Denial Letters ICD-9 Diagnosis Texts

Department	Critical Supplies List
Accounting	IBM XT
	IBM AT
	Panasonic Senior Partner
	PC Ribbons
Billing/Enrollment	Group and Individual Bills Forms
MIS	

2.0 Transportation Security Requirements

The following is a list of the security requirements by departments within HealthWays:

Department	Transportation Security
Member Services	Negligible
Health Services	None
Claims	Minimum level of protection and security
Accounting	No special level of protection or security is anticipated
Billing/Enrollment	Normal file level security
MIS	

3.0 Critical Number of Terminals

The following is the list of the critical number of terminals required by each department during the disaster period:

Department	Number of Terminals
Member Services	4
Health Services	4
Claims	Long-term use: 9
	Short-term use: 5

Department	Number of Terminals
Accounting	None
Billing/Enrollment	4
MIS	4

4.0 Special Reports

The following is a list of required special reports by departments. Those reports are defined as reports that MIS will develop and run for various departments if the online system could not be used for data capture during a disaster.

Department	Special Reports
Member Services	List of all active HealthWays subscribers
Health Services	List of eligible members
Claims	List of terminated subscribers and members
	List of new enrollees and effective dates
Accounting	None
Billing/Enrollment	None

5.0 Contracted for Reports

The following is a list of reports for which various departments within HealthWays are responsible and must be delivered to various parties by specified and contracted dates:

Department	Contracted for Reports
Member Services	None
Health Services	Inpatient utilization
	(Monthly and Weekly)
	Outstanding inpatient bills

Department	Contracted for Reports
Claims	Claims remittance advices (bimonthly) 15% withhold report (and/or check) Income reporting form
Accounting	Monthly financial reports
Billing/Enrollment	Revenue information (for accounting department)

F

Generating an Operating System after a Disaster

The following steps should be taken to bring up DOS/VSE after a disaster:

A. Using standalone fastcopy, restore dump, then back up tapes (most recent backup) onto DASD volumes.

B. Using standalone restore, restore the Sysres or IJSYSRS library to incorporate changes to ASIPROC (if at Comdisco) or put most recent copy of members in the library.

C. IPL the System from DOSRES (see note).

D. Before starting VTAM or CICS, you should do restore of private libraries, ICCF libraries, and VSAM files.

E. Bring up VTAM and CICS.

F. Logon to ICCF and BVSM.

Note: If you are at Comdisco, you may want to IPL the system with different IPL and JCL procedures. In that case, after executing IPL command, list the external interrupt key. You will get the following message: "ENTER SUPERVISOR PARAMETERS OR IPL PARAMETERS." You should reply as follows: IPL=$IPL —-, JCL=$$JCL where $IPL and $$JCL are the new procedure names cataloged in IJSYSRS.

2.0 Changes to Primary Site Operating System

The following changes should be made to the operating system at the primary site to create an operating system for Comdisco:

1. Modify ASIPROC to incorporate the following:

   A. IPL with supervisor having VM support.
   B. Paging to be handled by UM.
   C. Define all the devices that will be used at Comdisco.
   D. Change the name of IPL procedures and JCL so that they are different from those at primary site.
   E. Change the size, alloc. and allocr parameters for different partitions (if necessary).

2. Modify CICS tables as follows:

   A. Add or delete terminals on printers in your TCT that will be used at Comdisco.
   B. Assemble and linkedit table under a different table suffix.
   C. Include the above table in your CICS/ICCF startup deck and not in the regular TCT by overriding from the console or change the startup deck and leave in reader queue.

3. Modify VTAM books as follows:

   A. Modify your VTAM books defining the terminals and printers required at the recovery site.
   B. Modify your VTAM books for remote terminals to incorporate various macros used by NCP.
   C. Catalog above books in source statement library. Include above books in your startup books for VTAM.

Bibliography

Atre, S., *Data Base: Structured Techniques for Design, Performance, and Management*, J. Wiley & Sons, New York, 1988.

Brathwaite, K. S., *Analysis Design, and Implementation of Data Dictionaries*, McGraw-Hill, New York, 1988.

Brathwaite, K. S., *Data Administration*, J. Wiley & Sons, New York, 1985.

Brathwaite, K. S., "Management Involvement in Data Security, Integrity, and Privacy," AGT Tech. Memo, No. 15, 1980.

Brathwaite, K. S., "A Study of Data Base Security, Integrity and Privacy in a Large Public Utility," AGT Tech. Memo, No. 20, 1980.

Brathwaite, K. S., *Systems Design in DB Environment*, McGraw-Hill, New York, 1989.

Brown, D., "RACF — A Program to Enhance Security and Control," EDPACS, Vol. 6, No. 12, Institute of Internal Auditors, June 1979.

Brown, P. S., "Computer Security — A Survey," NCC, AFIPS Press, Washington, D.C., 1976.

Brown, P. S., *Security: Checklist for Computer Center Self-Audits*, AFIPS Press, Washington, D.C., 1979.

Chen, P. P., Ed, Proceedings of the International Conference on Entity-Relationship Approach to Systems Analysis and Design, North-Holland Publishing, New York, 1979.

Chen, P. P., Ed, Proceedings of the International Conference on Entity-Relationship Approach to Information Modelling and Analysis, North-Holland Publishing, New York, 1981.

Courtney, R. H., "Security Risk Assessment in Electronic Data Processing Systems," AFIPS Conf. Proc. 46, 1979, NCC 97–104, AFIPS Press, Washington, D.C., 1977.

Davenport, R. A., "Data Analysis for Database Design," *The Australian Computer Journal*, Vol. 10, No. 4, Brisbane, Australia, 1979, 122–137.

Dinardo, C. T., *Computers and Security*, AFIPS Press, Washington, D.C., 1978.

Durell, W. R., *Data Administration*, McGraw-Hill, New York, 1985.

Engelman, C., "Audit and Surveillance of Multi-level Computing Systems," MTR-3207, The Mitre Corporation, Washington, D.C., June 1975.

Fernandez, E. B., *Database Security and Integrity*, Addison-Wesley, New York, 1981.

Fosdick, H., *Using IBM's ISPF Dialog Manager*, Van Nostrand Reinhold, New York, 1987.

Gillenson, M., *Database: Step-by-Step*, J. Wiley & Sons, New York, 1985.

Gillenson, M., & Goldberg, R., *Strategic Planning Systems Analysis and Data Base Design*, J. Wiley & Sons, New York, 1984.

Hoffman, L. J., "The Formulary Model for Access Control and Privacy in Computer Systems," SCAC Report No. 119, Palo Alto, CA, May 1970.

Hsiao, D. K., *Computer Security*, Academic Press, Inc., San Diego, CA, 1979.

Hubbard, G., *Computer-Assisted Data Base Design*, Van Nostrand Reinhold, New York, 1981.

Kahn, B. K., "A Method for Describing the Information Required by the Data Base Design Process," Proc. Int. ACM/Sigmod Conf. Management of Data, New York, 1976.

Katzan, H., *Computer Data Security*, Van Nostrand Reinhold, New York, 1973.

Korth, H. F., and Silbersehatz, R., *Database System Concepts*, McGraw-Hill, New York, 1986.

Larson, B., *The Database Experts Guide to DB2*, McGraw-Hill, New York, 1988.

Lusardi, F., *The Database Experts Guide to SQL*, McGraw-Hill, New York, 1988.

Lusk, E. L., "A Practical Design Methodology for the Implementation of IMS Databases Using the E-R Model," ACM Vol. 4, New York, 1980, 9–21.

Martin, J., and McClure, C., *Structured Techniques: The Basis for CASE*, Prentice-Hall, Englewood Cliffs, NJ, 1988.

Novak, D., and Fry, J., "The State of the Art of Logical Database Design," Proc. 5th Texas Conf. Computing Systems (IEEE), Long Beach, CA, 1976.

Statland, N., "Data Security and Its Impact on EDP Auditing," EDPACS, Vol. 3, No. 4, Institute of Internal Auditors, New York, October 1979.

Weldon, J. L., *Database Administration*, Plenum Press, New York, 1981.

Whitmore, J. C., "Design for Multics Security Enhancements," ESD-TR-74-176, Honeywell Info. Systems, Palo Alto, CA, 1974.

Yao, S. B., "An Integrated Approach to Logical Database Design," NYU Symposium on Database Design, May 18–19, New York, 1978.

Index